The Art of Betrayal

Wanda R. Bishop

I0152055

Creative Touch Publishing LLC.

Creative Touch Publishing

1

Published by Creative Touch Publishing LLC.
P.O. Box 7482
Warner Robins, GA 31095
ctpublishing14@gmail.com
www.creativetouchpublishing.com

Printed and bound in the United States of America

1. Spiritual.   2. Motivational.   3. Non-Fiction.

International Standard Book Number

978-0-578-65648-9

CB TABLE OF CONTENTS CB

Dedication. 4

Encouraging Foreword. 6

Explanation of Book Cover. 9

Introduction. 15

Chapter 1: A Living Sacrifice (My Testimony) 19

Chapter 2: Betrayal – A Defining Moment. 41

Chapter 3: Betrayal in the Nest. 69

Chapter 4: A House Divided-Betrayal in the Church. . .97

Chapter 5: A Friend Should Love at All Times. 119

Chapter 6: The Fire is Necessary! 135

Chapter 7: F.O.C.U.S. 151

Chapter 8: If You Lose Your Life You Will Find It. 167

Conclusion. 177

ᘓ DEDICATION ᘓ

I dedicate these writings to my Heavenly Father, my Savior/Redeemer Jesus Christ, the Holy Spirit, and to you the reader who is struggling with betrayal and/or being an assailant. I thank God for His grace and mercies that are new every morning **(Lamentations 3:22-24).**

I am thankful for those who have influenced my life and helped me to learn, grow, and mature. To my parents, my husband Joey, our children, and grandchildren who are so encouraging.

I thank God for those who are assigned as my spiritual covering on this Christian journey; you are full of knowledge, wisdom, understanding and unconditional love.

One of my greatest inspiration besides Jesus Christ is my laid to rest, beautiful paternal grandmother; Mary Frances Jones King. I admired my grandmother very much as she taught me so much while fishing, sitting under her big oak tree, sitting on her huge porch shucking corn or peeling peas and keeping an eye on my aunt Michelle; her disabled daughter who was around my age.

My grandmother Frances birthed 15 children with 14 surviving; she scuffled taking care of several grandchildren, a house, a side cleaning job while still taking the time to have fun with us playing kick ball and such.

I now realize at the age of 50 that I possess many of my grandmother's virtues. Love, hope, peace, and strength were instilled in me at an early age. Grandmother would take in anything stray; people, animals, you name it.

I regret that she passed away due to alcoholism. It took her body while she was in her mid-50's. "But God," our Heavenly Father rescued her soul after she gave her life to Jesus prior to her passing, and I am looking forward to seeing her again.

෬ENCOURAGING FOREWORD ෬

My wife Wanda, is one of the most amazing and strong-willed women and mothers I have ever known. She has a heart of gold and will help anyone in need. After over 31 years of marriage I am still in love with her. She is my soulmate and angel sent by God and I will love her forever.

Always my love: Hubby Joey

My mother has done the impossible in my eyes, and of course she gives the credit to Jesus. Mom is an amazing woman of prayer who doesn't take any mess. I have learned to be kind to others because of the example she has given me as her son and for that, I am forever grateful.

I Love You Mom: Son Chris

My mother, "the embodiment of unwavering strength, of quietness, and confidence." Her life path and obstacles therein has given her the fearlessness and fortitude I admire so much. Mom has consistently nourished the lives of many throughout her journey. I believe that the light of your test and triumph will perpetually shine for generations to come.

The best Mom/Nanna ever: Daughter Velisha

Throughout my life, my mother has been so much to me; mainly a teacher. She has taught me how to make wise decisions; even in the times of trouble. Mom is a faithful Christian, dedicated employee, and a wife of honesty, encouragement, and strength. Everything I have watched you go through has made living my life easier. I appreciate you as a mother who made mistakes but has done her best to correct and repair.

Blessings Mother; Daughter Lakendra

I have known my dearest sister in Christ for nearly two decades. It has been a pleasure to work with her in ministry and an honor to watch her grow in the faith. It is awesome that God has given her the strength and peace to chronicle her amazing weights. He caused what was meant for evil to blossom into an inspiring testimony.

Expect Greatness; Dr. Dan Solomon

I love my sister from another mother. You are my prayer warrior who took me under your wing as a friend and co-worker with the Sheriffs' Department. Wanda is such a kind hearted person and a true woman of faith whom I can always call upon to encourage and lift my spirit. I know that this book is going to bless your life simply because of who she is.

Go for it, my Dear Friend; Kassie Taylor

This book is inspired by a wonderfully anointed woman of God, who has overcome many trying times in her life. She is the proof in the pudding of what it really means to remain steadfast; even in difficult time. Reading this book will reassure you that if God has seen her through, He can and will do the same for you. This is a must read!

Bishop Harvey and Dr. Veronica Bee
The Winning Church, Warner Robins, GA

❧ EXPLANATION OF BOOK ❧ COVER

The Lord advised me to design this book using the following colors: scarlet, blue, purple, and gold accented with fire. The fire represents the Holy Spirit who burns away all types of sin from our lives.

Scarlet represents the sins we have committed and shows how the enemy would dare to put a mark upon our life, "But God."

Blue, reminds us of Gods' promises of eternal life and of His earthly blessings as we look up toward the lovely blue sky. Purple reminds us that, as converted Christians, God clothed us with royalty when we repented, accepted his inheritance, and were redeemed by Him. His word tells us that the earth is His and the fullness thereof, the world and they that dwell therein **(Psalms 24:1).**

Gold is to remind us of how beautiful and royal God is. He tells us in His word that the great or main street of the city in heaven is as pure gold **(Revelation 21:21).** The colors blue, purple, gold and scarlet are found throughout the bible. A look at **Exodus 25:4** shows where God told Moses to receive offerings which included blue, purple, and scarlet yarn, as well as gold and many other gifts. Those items were fine materials which were used by the Israelites; Gods chosen people.

In **Exodus 28:15** we see again where certain materials were chosen to be valuable and were to be used to make a breastplate shaped like an ephod. Those materials included gold, blue, purple and scarlet yarn.

In **Exodus 36:8** the bible shows where the tabernacle was hung with linen curtains of blue, purple and scarlet. In **Exodus 36:37** the entrance of the Tabernacle of Moses was covered with gold, blue, purple, and scarlet once again.

God could have chosen any other colors, as there are so many, but he chose the four listed here to make His presence known. Scarlet, in the bible, was used to describe some of the fine materials and threads. It was also used in Mosaic purification rituals. Scarlet, like crimson, is used to describe sin and it generally symbolizes a marker as some would look at the color scarlet as one who practices abominable sins.

God used this mark to show how mighty he really is. He confused religious systems and saved those that were marked with scarlet; such as Rahab.

She hung a scarlet rope from the window to help the spies in **Joshua 1:15-21**.

In **Joshua chapter 2** Rahab, a woman who lived as a prostitute, recognized the power of God and, though her sins were as scarlet, God points her out as an example of obedience. We may look at her in a negative light but God used her as an example because she recognized His power. Through her obedience both she and her household were saved.

Isaiah 1:18-20 tells us that we can be saved from our sins, the destruction of hell, and be blessed if we are willing to obey. *Come now, and let us reason together, "Says the LORD, "Though your sins are like scarlet, They shall be as white as snow; Though they are red like crimson, They shall be as wool.[19] If you are willing and obedient, You shall eat the good of the land; [20] But if you refuse and rebel, You shall be devoured by the sword"; For the mouth of the LORD has spoken.*

In **Proverbs 31:21** the virtuous woman clothes her household with scarlet. Hebrews 9:19 shares how scarlet, wool, along with blood, and other items were chosen by Moses to make a blood covenant with our Heavenly Father.

The color scarlet symbolizes our sins and is mentioned throughout the Bible, but Jesus came to wash away all sin and He remembers them no more. They have been thrown in the depths of the sea. We were not created to sin but to worship and obey God.

Blue or sapphire, my favorite color, is a representation of the heavenlies. This can be found in **Exodus 24:10** and in **Ezekiel 1:26, 10:1** where the glory of the Lord clothed in sapphire was above the cherubim. Blue also represents a holy service. We find this in **Exodus 28:31** where a priestly robe was worn by Aaron before entering a holy place.

Mordecai went out from the presence of the king wearing royal garments of blue and white, with a great crown of gold, and a purple robe of fine linen (**Esther 8:15)**. Purple became a symbol of royalty and riches due to the scarcity of its dye. **II Chronicles 2:7; Ezekiel 27:16; Acts 16:14 and Revelation 18:12** all provide descriptions of the dye trade.

The fire is a type of purification. God himself is a consuming fire **(Hebrews 12:29)** and certainly, He, the Lord of Lord, and King of Kings, Jesus Christ is pure; free from moral fault and guilt. He is ritually clean. All throughout the book of Exodus animals such as bulls, lambs, rams, and other sacrificial offerings were burned with fire before being presented to the Lord. Because of **Malachi 3:1-3** we recognize and understand that Jesus is coming as a refiner's fire to purify and to purge; in order to bring righteousness. In **Genesis 19:1-26** we see that the Lord rained down fire and brimstone in order to destroy the wicked cities where men desired to lay with men. The Lord only spared those who were righteous and pure in His sight.

ॐ INTRODUCTION ॐ

The artwork on the book cover depicting a
sword with the colors blue, purple, and scarlet red is
used as a representation of our blood. Being cut, both
spiritually and naturally, is not all bad if we look at it
through the eyes of Jesus. The cutting may cause pain
and feelings of betrayal, and one may think that this is a
malicious act to cause hurt or possible death, but often
times it is very necessary in our lives. One reference of
cutting in the Bible is known as circumcision; a cutting
away of the foreskin on males to prevent infection. In
some countries, such as Africa, this practice also
includes the clitoris of a female.

Circumcision was known in the Jewish culture
but today males in America are circumcised to prevent
infection. I don't believe a sword was used but perhaps
some type of knife or sharp object. I use a sword in this
illustration, as a representation of spiritual cutting. It

depicts the sword of the spirit mentioned in **Ephesians 6:17** and in **Hebrews 4:12.**

Hebrews 4:12 says; *for the word of God is alive and powerful. It is sharper than the sharpest two-edged sword, cutting between soul and spirit, between joint and marrow. It exposes our innermost thoughts and desires.*

God's word is so powerful and capable of exposing the things we as human-beings fail to see in the natural. The supernatural power of the Holy Spirit can easily reveal within our hearts. The cutting we experience from the word is not in vain; it prevents infection, disease, and contamination of the heart and to others. **Romans 2:25-29** explains the importance of circumcision and how the law of circumcision is basically just a custom or tradition.

[24]For circumcision is indeed profitable if you keep the law; but if you are a breaker of the law, your circumcision has become uncircumcision. [25]Therefore, if an uncircumcised man keeps the righteous requirements of the law, will not his uncircumcision be counted as circumcision? [27] And will not the physically uncircumcised, if he fulfills the

law, judge you who, even with your written code and
circumcision, are a transgressor of the law? ²⁸ For he
is not a Jew who is one outwardly, nor is circumcision
that which is outward in the flesh; ²⁹
but he is a Jew who is one inwardly; and circumcision
is that of the heart, in the Spirit, not in the letter;
whose praise is not from men but from God.

Romans 2:25-29 (NKJV)

My goal in providing this explanation of why cutting is necessary, is to prevent contamination and infection. If our hearts are contaminated, it is difficult to prosper in life according to God's will. The cutting is also necessary to deal with high-mindedness; whether for those of us who may think too highly of ourselves; believer or not. We tend to get high-minded, puffed up, and prideful, presenting a need to be cut back before we end in destruction and miss our purpose on the earth and in eternity. Our goal should be to see Jesus and hear Him say, "well done thou good and faithful servant."

Some of us like praises from man (the people we are around) more than that from our creator, but our desire should never be to please people or seek their approval. If we please our Father in Heaven, then we will experience favor from man. Most of us want "right now blessings" and "right now rewards," but often times, we are not prepared for them. Sometimes we experience a cut that may seem deep; that we think we are going to bleed forever, but the bleeding caused by the cut may be what cleanses us so that purification and healing can take place. Someone once said, "What doesn't kill us can only make us stronger."

CHAPTER ONE

A Living Sacrifice (My Testimony)
Romans 12:1-2

This chapter was a very difficult one for me to share, so much so, that I didn't want to share it at all. However, as a Christian, I realized a long time ago that I am bought with a price and no longer my own.

I was also inspired by a dear friend and author; Thedoshia L. Shealey as she states in "The Power to Overcome Fear," that God has given each of us as a believer a specific task to accomplish, but because of fear, we choose to run the other way. I finally realized that it was time to stop running from the call on my life. "The Power to Overcome Fear" explains how we should ignore the lies of the enemy who desires to stop us with fear from reaching our God divine potential in order to be a blessing to others. Although some of you may be very critical and judgmental, I believe others will be very blessed and experience a miraculous breakthrough.

I am very grateful to God for the many ways He has used me in this life. He has added chapters of triumph, failure, faith, hardship, friendship, achievements and so on. I share this testimony not to boast or brag, but to share how good God has been to me; He is my everything. I boast solely in Jesus; the author and finisher of my faith. My main purpose for publicly sharing such intimate details is to help others know and understand that you can do all things through Christ who gives you strength. Regardless of the type of pain you have experienced, whether it be through betrayal or at your own hands, with you being the assailant. Know there is hope and it is everlasting as long as you put your hope in Jesus who gives us the capabilities to do the impossible.

Some of us have experienced impossibilities, while others, who may or may not have a relationship with the Father; find it is hard to believe that our creator can do anything. I know some of you are really struggling with past hurt, pain, and disappointment. I know the feeling, as I have not always been as stable, triumphant, or courageous enough to accomplish anything on my own. It has been by the grace of God and the wonderful people He put in my path; such as clergy, teachers, friends, and family encouraging me along the way.

The enemy had a plan to destroy me; he tried to

kill me in several ways shortly after I was born. My mother nearly died giving birth to me, and if that wasn't enough, I experienced so much physical, emotional, sexual, and mental abuse as a child, I remember wanting to die on several occasions; "But God."

I am led to share the tragedies of betrayal I have suffered, as well as my experiences as an assailant. It began with what seemed like a curse from the very beginning of my childhood. Growing up in a house of five and being the only dark child in the household was difficult. I had to deal with individuals saying that I was adopted, switched at birth, had a different father than my siblings and that my mother had to have slept with one of my uncles, who was my complexion, because I looked so much like my grandmother. Because I was very active and creative as a child, I was able to block out the negativity and immerse myself into others things. Most of the time I lived in a fantasy world just to escape the pain.

The physical abuse started at the age of six while I was in the first grade. It stemmed from a very mean teacher who was racist. She beat me daily. Being the only dark child in the classroom, students used the "N" word quite frequently; I remember crying and sleeping a lot. The teacher purposely seated me in the very back of the room so she wouldn't have to interact with me.

The most hurtful thing I remember happened during the holidays. Parents often brought special snacks to share with the children during Christmas, Easter, and on Valentine's Day. My teacher would purposely skip over me, sometimes telling the parents that I did not deserve anything.

Because the teacher ignored me, I would often force myself to sleep until it was either lunchtime or time to go home. On one occasion I remember being awakened and forced out into the hallway where I was beaten with a paddle for no apparent reason. This confused and angered me.

Mom loved to send us looking pretty in our dresses, so when the beatings occurred in first grade, I was practically spanked on a bare bottom.

By the time I reached 2nd grade, I was a very angry and spiteful child with major behavior problems. My 2nd grade teacher, who was a young African American woman, had no clue what to do with me so, once again, she seated me in the back of the classroom away from the other students. By the end of my 2nd grade year I showed no academic progress so I had to repeat it. This time I was assigned to a teacher named Mrs. Ash.

Although I had behavior issues, Mrs. Ash didn't tolerate it. She refused to allow me to sleep and not learn. Mrs. Ash was tough and persistent yet caring, consistent, and genuine. If I slept during instruction time, she would take away my recess and spend one on one time with me. Mrs. Ash refused to allow me to act out or have my way but when I did well, she rewarded and encourage me to keep it up and that seemed strange to me.

I began to enjoy learning and was eventually able to have the same privileges as the other children. I advanced to the 3rd grade and remember feeling really good about my accomplishment. While in 3rd grade around the age of 9, I started noticing that something was not right with my mother. I began seeing all sorts of bruises and scars on her body and later learned that domestic violence had creeped its ugly head into my home.

My mother was a stay at home mom who took great care of the home but was often attacked by her spouse and in-laws. Nearing the 4th grade, I began to get consumed with my mother's problems and felt like I had to stay close to her. All I ever saw was her cooking and cleaning the house and preparing for her special weekends. On certain weekends, mom made extra money selling certain hot dishes, such as fish, chicken, pork chops, barbecue sandwiches, and Brunswick stew and many other items to her customers.

I recall seeing all sorts of people attending my mom's special events. One weekend in particular sticks out to me that I thought was strange. I remember at one of the gatherings, watching two relatives staring at me in a way that made me very nervous. I overheard them whispering things that were sexual in nature. As a child, I didn't understand their plot to harm me, but not long after that evening I became a victim of molestation and sexual abuse.

The act took place nearly every weekend and I was told by one of them that I had better not tell anyone. I was scared, confused, and had no idea how I could even begin to let someone know what was going on; because we were not taught good touch or bad touch. By the time I was 11 years old, the abuse became a normal part of my life, I expected it, cooperated, cried, then went into my fantasy world to escape the pain. The only person who knew what was going on was my younger sister closest to me. I tried to convince her to steal our dad's shot-gun so I could kill my abusers. My sister tried convincing me to tell mom or someone, but I was too afraid and felt that everyone had their own problems to deal with. I escaped the pain by playing my trombone outside under our large oak tree; that was my sanctuary.

I pretended to be a band director, often imagining I was directing an orchestra. I had developed a love for music as I wrote music and even formed a little band with my brother and two uncles who were around my age. We even performed a few times for the guests who gathered at our house on the weekends.

By the time I was 12 years old I had become numb to the abuse and due to my creativity, I thought I was providing a service that I should get paid for; one of my abusers agreed. I received money and drove his car whenever I wanted. Around the age of 12 ½ my mother caught one of the molesters in the act and decided to move us away.

Starting over in a new community was very difficult for me. We lived with one relative after another until mom was approved for low income housing. I hated trying to make new friends but at least I felt safe. One issue I faced after the move was that my new school was rivals with my old school. They didn't welcome me right away, but my athletic and music abilities helped me obtain favor. Sexual abuse causes so much harm, and when the assailant is a family member, I believe the damage is far worse than anyone can imagine. I grew up not being able to interact with the opposite sex; at one point hated the site of men. Being the person that I am, I decided to give a guy a try.

My first relationship did not last very long due to him talking about hurting me physically, because I would not cooperate with his sexual desires. As a result, I decided to just be alone and focus on school, reaching my goals, and fulfilling my dream of becoming a military police officer. I was now 16 years old, "But God."

One day at the age of 17, one of my cousins wanted to visit an old classmate who had recently given birth to a baby girl. Since my cousin didn't know how to drive, she asked me to take her to see her friend. While standing outside admiring the baby; my cousins' friend, had a brother who pulled up in his car and requested that I move my car so he could park around back, so I allowed him to. I continued admiring the baby while my back was turned and did not notice this guy standing behind me in the yard until the others started laughing and looking past me. I turned and saw this skinny guy checking me out. I immediately thought, such a pervert. Being embarrassed, I decided to wait on my cousin in the car. While walking to my car this guy insisted on getting my phone number, although I refused, he found another way to get me to go out with him. After about two years we had a son and got married. Although Joey has been very good to me, I tested his love for me on every hand, and no matter what, he remained that gentle, kind, and generous man I love dearly today.

As the years passed, I became more knowledgeable and learned that the testing of my husband's love, as well as from others, stemmed from the sexual and physical abuse I'd suffered. Because of the history of sexual abuse, I struggled with intimacy, establishing a connection, and experiencing true love. I longed to connect and feel what my husband felt but there was a blockage in my heart that only Jesus could fix. Our marriage struggled and I began to search for pleasure in all the wrong places; alcohol, other men, parties, and such. The infidelity began to destroy our relationship; I had become too carefree in our marriage. I betrayed my husband several times and every time he forgave me, even after having someone else's child. I have no doubt that my husband's love is a type of Christ.

I began to search for a better life and gave my life to Jesus. I remember crying out to God after nearly 7 years of marriage. As a Christian, I placed my trust in God who said He could do anything, and guess what...He did it!

The supernatural power of God brought forth such breakthrough time of intimacy, the experience and connection were amazing. I tried to run from my husband but God knew who and what I needed to get a breakthrough and experience the unconditional love He wanted me to have.

I was ashamed to tell my husband about my past, so I withheld it. This is not wise entering into a marriage. It is best to be open and honest with your potential spouse and seek counseling if necessary.

You are probably wondering if my husband found out about the abuse. Joey learned about the abuse from a potential foster parent questionnaire I had left on the kitchen table. After I returned from the restroom, we talked about the incident and that is when I began to explain the previous times when I was so timid, shameful, and afraid. I apologized for not telling him and explained that I also did not want to be treated like a victim.

Intimacy in a marriage between a man and a woman should be to the glory of God, honorable, pleasurable, joyful, and free. I am so thankful that God allowed me to experience such an awesome gift between my husband and I. We were able to be naked and not ashamed, as a result we were able to bring forth life.

Keep in mind; I do not share this to gain sympathy, empathy, or to try and impress you, but to encourage those who have been or are going through similar situations, and perhaps don't know which way to turn. I am reminded that God is Alpha and Omega, He has been by my side my entire life.

When God's hands are on you, there is no way any environment can destroy what He is doing in your life. I am fortunate to know God's sovereignty. When I became a Christian, I thanked Him for breaking the curse. I share these difficult times with you as the reader to encourage your heart and reassure you that all things are possible with God. I no longer live in the past and am grateful to God for allowing me to experience the present with family, friends, and others I have met along the way. Because I had low self-esteem and such low self-worth, I really didn't know who I was. I acted out of character and was unfaithful in my marriage. Due to my husband's work schedule and our children being small, I often found myself alone. It was during that time that I began operating as an assailant without realizing it. Depression and loneliness led me to a place of self- destruction; "But God!"

I recall a time when I worked as a young manager at Robins AFB. There was an older guy who constantly harassed me sexually. My husband was in training out of the state at the time and, for some crazy reason, I thought that if I just slept with him once he would leave me alone and get off of my back. My analogy worked, he left me alone but, although I used protection, I miraculously became pregnant for him. My husband returned home days later and we were intimate. I never imagined I would get pregnant for another man.

Twelve years later I discovered that our baby girl was from another man. This was revealed to me while listening to a minister on a CD preach about secret sins. I remember telling myself that I don't have to worry about any secret sins; until the Holy Spirit said, "look at your youngest daughter." I looked at her and remember saying, "no way God, I used protection with that guy but she looks just like him. Oh God, what am I going to do." My husband came into the kitchen and saw a strange look on my face and I immediately felt the need to lay down. He followed me into the bedroom demanding to know what was wrong but I told him that we needed to talk to the Pastor or someone to seek counseling. He continued to demand an answer, that's when I told him what I was thinking and feeling. He immediately shook it off like it was nothing until about an hour later; then it was as if the devil himself showed up. I had become an assailant to my family due to infidelity which resulted in a child. There was an abundance of pain and deep betrayal,
"But God!"

My husband and I were contemplating a

divorce when our daughter began saying she felt like she was adopted. She wondered why children at school would say things about her not looking like her siblings. The situation caused a lot of confusion in our household; the enemy thought that he was wreaking havoc. Because my husband and I were at odds with one another the children pressured me for answers. I told them that in time, God would work it out. I informed our Pastor of what was going on and, one day after asking how things were going between us, he told me to keep praying.

God is Able: A Ram in the Bush

In spite of my husband and I passing one another through the house for nearly two weeks without talking, God was still working. One Saturday, the girls were invited to a sleepover and my husband decided to take them; it was pouring down rain. I was resting after work but still praying and fasting. I noticed that my husband and the girls had been gone for quite some time so I called our friend to see if they had made it to their house; which was only about 20 minutes away. Our friends stated that they were not there.

The Mrs. of the house asked if I wanted her to send her husband out to look for them but I replied, "no, let's wait a few more minutes due to the bad storm." I was a police officer at the time, and felt that if something had happened I would more than likely have been contacted since the van was in my name. Shortly after hanging up the phone, I heard my husband in the driveway and noticed that he was under the hood of our new van. I asked him what was going on and he informed me that as soon as they got near the Downers' house, the van just cut off on its own. He told me that he had checked everything while stopped on the side of the road and that there seemed to have been nothing wrong with it, so he and the girls just sat in the van on the side of the road.

Joey had to work that night so I didn't get in his way, but he said he was going to drive the van to work to make sure everything was okay.

The next morning was our sons' birthday. I got prepared to let him spend it the way he had asked; shopping, then with one of his best friends. After dropping Christopher off, I returned home to change into my uniform and get ready for work. There in my patrol car, I found a long letter with flowers and gifts that drew me to tears. Joey explained to me that he believed it was God who stopped the van and allowed the girls to give him a scowling lecture concerning our marriage. He explained that the girls preached to him about forgiveness and expressed how much I loved him. They encouraged him to apologize for his actions. I went inside the house and Joey greeted me at the door with open arms. We apologized to one another and I told him I would be working a short detail and would return home swiftly. A year later, our family began improving as we turned to one another for encouragement and talked things out within our home.

I reached out for advice from an unknown spiritual counselor who reassured me that healing takes time. During that year we experienced a miraculous breakthrough, then the enemy rose up in our home once again.

Rumors were spreading amongst the teens and young adults. I instructed our girls to stay out of the confusion but unfortunately, busy-bodies, persisted in keeping up the confusion.

One night, we experienced what I thought was an act of betrayal that was sure to kill us; not necessarily because of this one act but because we were already dealing with so many other issues. The rumors involved our youngest daughter and it turned out that we were the sermon topic that night. We were publicly humiliated and verbally attacked; it was like a nightmare. As this was going on, I sat there thinking, "how evil; how could someone allow the enemy to use them in this manner without knowing the facts.

Matthew 18:15-17 tells us that when there is an issue amongst Christians, we are supposed to try and resolve those issues in private, then if that doesn't work, we should try to resolve the matter with another witness present before making it public. My attempts were to no avail; no one listened.

The attack caused our daughter to slip into a suicidal state; she began physically harming herself. I was unaware of it until Ms. Desiree, a school counselor and friend informed me to discreetly keep a very close watch on her. I asked God, why is this happening to us? We didn't deserve such treatment. We hold no grudges towards anyone, and I am only sharing this to help you understand that betrayal comes in many forms, but you do not have to allow it to prosper and ruin your life.

Although this was a very difficult time for us at

this particular ministry, there were some very rewarding times of friendship and love. It is the enemy who comes to steal, kill, and destroy and all of us are guilty of being used by the devil.

When things become so difficult that it seems as if there is no way to work things out, know that it is okay to move on. It's ok to move forward in another relationship, it is okay to move forward in another job, another goal, even another ministry, and that's exactly what we did. I am very grateful we decided to relocate to another church; it was for the sake of healing our family. The new church had an awesome youth pastor who had a heart for young people. He challenged our daughter to be better than the pain.

Betrayal is real and can be hurtful, but it is still a part of life. I have experienced wrongful terminations, public humiliation, discrimination, racism, and sexism, rejection from friends and family members, unexpected deaths of loved ones, physical and sexual attacks...you name it, but those things do not define who we truly are.

Another act of betrayal was when I found out that one of the individuals who sexually attacked me as a child, had struck again. I was very hurt and felt that I had failed those individuals by not coming forth previously. I am not sharing this information to hurt or embarrass anyone and I have concluded that revealing names is unnecessary, but when things like this happen, it must be dealt with immediately.

Looking back over my life, I am very grateful to be alive, sane, and as a Christian, bearing the fruit of the Spirit. After reading this testimony, many would say that I have every reason to be totally opposite, "But God."

The devil tried to kill me, my marriage, my children, my career, and my destiny, but God was not having it. I am so thankful to God for putting loving teachers, wise spiritual leaders, friends, a loving mother, grandmother, husband, and children in my life. They taught me the meaning of unconditional love!

I am thankful for the individuals God has allowed me to influence within my home, careers, areas of service and volunteering within my church. He has allowed me to teach, change lives, and make a difference in society; all while being led by the Holy Spirit and sharing love with those who have struggled with similar issues.

I urge you to keep striving, it's worth the fight,

my family is a living witness, as we have experienced so much. Each of us have been on both sides of the coin; being betrayed as well as being the assailant, but God has and is pulling us through.

Another act of betrayal occurred when I teamed up with a family member in a business, which I was the primary owner of. As a result of his negligence, other family members were able to steal over $35,000 from the business account. I could go on and on about the struggles, trials, and tests I have endured but I must admit, what didn't kill me has made me stronger, better, and wiser.

One of the main lessons I have learned through it all is that I can dry my tears and show the devil that he cannot and will not win...no matter what. Don't be a casualty of the enemy, he has no more power than you allow him to have. Don't be a victim, you are victorious...stay that way!

After Jesus captured my heart, I became a very free-spirited individual; full of life, dreams, vision, and perseverance. I came to realize that those qualities were there the whole time. Spiritually, I now realize that numerous demonic weapons were forming against me at an early age in an attempt to stop God's plan for my life, "But God."

I am so grateful for determining to stay alive, to persevere, and be a blessing to others. I have learned that not everyone will accept you or understand your path in life. You have to be okay with that, and know that as long as Jesus accepts you; that is all that matters. One thing is certain, if an individual or group rejects you for whatever reason, God is able to surround you with others who know how to receive and love you where you are. If I had chosen to die rather than live, I would have missed out on so much that life had to offer.

In the next few chapters I will share more on how to be an overcomer after experiencing betrayal, and/or being an assailant. Remember, nothing is too hard for God!

C3 CHAPTER TWO C3

Betrayal: A Defining Moment

When I think of art; something or someone that is created from an imagination, a vision, or from within comes to mind. Merriam Webster defines "art" as "a skill acquired by experience, study, or observation. It is further defined as, "a branch of learning, as, "one of the humanities, and as a conscious use of skill and creative imagination." Art must be created by an artist, a skilled performer, or one who is adept to something. The word "**adept**" should be kept in mind as it may help you in your journey to healing, deliverance, and ultimately into a place of freedom. Art is created or fashioned by an artist.

The art of betrayal requires skill; experience. It is often learned by observation and is a part of humanity. When we think of humanity, of course we think of humans; mankind, or the flesh. As believers, we should always be aware that operating in the flesh gets us into trouble. Enough about the word art, let's consider the word betrayal.

Betrayal can occupy our members, (the mind, the body, soul, and spirit) through various ways.

1. **Through Experience**: When it comes to our bodies, we may try something and enjoy the results, however, attempting the same thing at a different time may yield unfavorable results; not working out the way we anticipated.

2. **Through Learned Behavior**: Learned behaviors are developed and established in our minds, and usually stem from those within our immediate environments. This includes our parents, friends, teachers, and close relatives. We must use caution when it comes to learned behaviors because, if not careful, they can become deeply embedded habits and form generational curses.

3. **Through Human Nature**: Our flesh causes us to desire what is naturally pleasurable. If left unchecked, it results in contamination. Oftentimes, we don't understand the amount of damage we cause others as a result of our own selfish fulfillments, so we do it anyway.

Biblical examples of this are Adam and Eve in the Garden of Eden **(Genesis 3:1-6, 16-19)** and David with Bathsheba **(2 Samuel 11:2-5, 1417, 26-27; 12:15-23).**

Webster defines the words betray or betrayal as, "to lead astray; to fail or desert in time of need; to reveal unintentionally; to disclose in violation of confidence."

The act of betrayal usually results in there being a victim. A victim is one who has been acted upon and adversely affected by a force or agent. It is one who is injured, destroyed, or sacrificed under any of variety of conditions. In the act of betrayal, there is also an assailant; one who has caused harm to another, either emotionally, physically, or both. This can cause spiritual instability.

Assailant may be a harsh word but when we are betrayed, we feel as though we have been violently attacked; as though our hearts have been ripped out. When considering various actions an individual may take to betray you, it is human nature to want revenge. The very act can leave one feeling worthless, defeated, helpless, and hurt in the deepest sense.

Oftentimes, victims become vindictive and attempt to handle matters in his or her own way, not realizing that the one who hurt them, or the assailant, may be wounded, and experiencing grief themselves. It is a proven fact that hurting people are inclined to hurt others without realizing it.

There are individuals who prey on others for personal gain; I am not referring to those types of people who are considered **divest** and also need help, but to those who act out of impulse, based on their pain, emotions, or perhaps learned behaviors. These types of individuals tend to cause pain for others and often don't know or understand why. The individuals I am referencing have a conscious but need a spiritual heart transplant. A curse needs to be broken off their lives and serious deliverance needs to take place.

I truly believe that love, trust, and respect, must be restored for an individual to be delivered from the effects of betrayal. For true restoration to take place, I believe that the relationship must be orchestrated through Jesus. It doesn't matter how many times we go to church, pray or operate in a spiritual gifting; the bottom line is that our heart needs to be fixed and no one can do that but Jesus. Once deliverance takes place, God can clean up the mess caused by the assailant if he or she allows him to. He can and will restore broken relationships. I am a living testimony that he can repair anything that is broken if we allow Him; He knows the intent of our hearts.

Whether you identify as the victim or the assailant, you must deal with your own feelings and self-worth so that you do not bleed or throw blame on others. Destruction lies within the soul of an individual who chooses not to deal with the pain and effects of betrayal. God can repair our hearts daily by teaching us to love ourselves again. He can teach those who have injured us, and those we have injured to forgive and learn to love ourselves, all while building our relationship with Jesus Christ.

Victims who experience betrayal are prone to suffer additional hardships, sometimes in the form of sickness or disease, if they do not release or forgive the individual who offended them. I can testify that my life, both naturally and spiritually have been bountifully blessed after I released liars, abusers, and other offenders while in a season of pain. As I stated earlier, hurt people tend to hurt others. It is always best to deal with our own issues before trying to assist others.

Failure to do so may result in additional chaos, confusion, and ultimately contamination of the one(s) we are trying to help.

Individuals who have experienced sexual, mental, physical, or emotional abused often portray this behavior both inside and outside of the home. This produces additional hurting people who, in turn, have a higher risk of hurting or victimizing others.

Most behaviors are learned through experience. For example, if a child is taught that stealing is okay, he or she will take things that do not belong to them without thinking twice about it. If incest, sexual, or physical abuse is a normal occurrence in the home, siblings or relatives usually pass this behavior on to their children and other relationships. Boys who witness their fathers beat their mothers and sexually abuse their sisters, perhaps them as well, may continue this cycle of abuse within their own families.

Having worked with adolescents and youth, for over 25 years now, has equipped me to easily identify what a child is taught or being exposed to. It is often revealed by their overall behavior toward others outside of the home. I am knowledgeable of juveniles who have committed some of the most unforgiving and malicious crimes, primarily due to the type of environment they were exposed to. Children are constantly influence by their normal surroundings.

I believe if we surround them with love, the proper attention, and instill the values and beliefs of Jesus Christ, we will have done our part in forming a wholesome well-behaved individual who will not prey on others. Real love doesn't prey on others.

When we hear how someone has violated another person through molestation, rape, murder, or by other means, we tend to label them as sick, disgusting, and insane. We usually feel that those who do such things should be tortured in the same manner. I don't believe that is the correct approach as the Lord has said that all souls are His **(Ezekiel 18:4).**

Don't get it twisted or confused, I am a firm believer that individuals who commit such crimes should be punished, but if all souls belong to God, He is the ultimate judge. It is He who decides whether to sentence them to Hell, or, if they turn from their wickedness, accept them into His Kingdom.

Sometimes we judge others so harshly, when in actuality; if we were to look in the mirror, we would see that we are or were, at some point in our lives, hell bound and not deserving of God's mercy and grace.

Behold, all souls are mine; as the soul of the father, so also the soul of the son is mine: the soul that sinneth, it shall die (Ezekiel 18:4 KJV).

Individuals who have evil spirits need Jesus just as much as anyone else and HE is where their help and deliverance lies. God created all man-kind. Of course, He did not create us to harm one another. Those who do are often acting out of victimization and repeating a learned behavior, which became a cycle that cursed their lives. Although these things do happen, there is hope if we, as Christians, are willing to share the Christ in us, who is the hope of glory **(Colossians 1:27)**.

The cycle of hurting others has to stop and Jesus is the one to break the cycle and free us from the curse(s) in which we suffer from generation to generation. We must allow Him to come into our hearts and repair us from within.

Victims often allow sickness, disease, oppression, mistreatment, attacks, and among other things humiliation to take control of their lives.

Understand that you don't have to remain a victim. You can be victorious in Jesus! He is the healer and deliverer who sets us free.

I am reminded of a saying that my mother often used when I was a child. There were times when I would strike back if someone attacked me, and she would say, "two wrongs won't make it right," which simply means that someone needs to forgive and not retaliate after they've been wronged. We must use wisdom in every situation because sometimes an individual need to be brought to justice, in such cases; we must allow the court to decide and administer the proper sanctions.

The bible speaks of many who were persecuted for righteousness sake. Some of us that think we are victims being persecuted for righteousness sake so that an exceeding weight of glory may be revealed through us during these light afflictions **(2 Corinthians 4:17).**

According to the bible, Jesus, Moses, Daniel, Job, and many others were mistreated and, even today, some have become martyrs for the sake of the gospel.

John was beheaded just for telling individuals to repent and change from their wicked ways.

Some people are divinely appointed to walk the path that Jesus walked, not necessarily to be crucified in the flesh but with him in the spirit; this may hurt our flesh dearly, but God knows how much we can handle. Jesus is not asking us to get on a cross, just to take up our cross and follow him.

If we follow Him, we will certainly experience persecution even from amongst our brethren just as he did. It is not easy being like Jesus, as God commands us to be, but in the end, it is worth it as He promises to give us an expected end **(Jeremiah 29:11)** along with eternal life.

The Word of God teaches us that we must endure hardness as good soldiers of Jesus Christ **(2 Timothy 2:3)**. We are supposed to go through this life as soldiers with the expectation of knowing that if He (Jesus), d doesn't save us; He is still able to do exceedingly abundantly above all that we ask or think according to the power that works in us **(Ephesians 3:20). I encourage you to count it all joy and hold on to your faith as you allow His power to work through you.**

John 3:14-21 makes it plain enough for anyone to see from the Message Bible:

14-15 "In the same way that Moses lifted the serpent in the desert so people could have something to see and then believe, it is necessary for the Son of Man to be lifted up—and everyone who looks up to him, trusting and expectant, will gain a real life, eternal life. 16-18 This is how much God loved the world: He gave his Son, his one and only Son. And this is why: so that no one need be destroyed; by believing in him, anyone can have a whole and lasting life. God didn't go to all the trouble of sending his Son merely to point an accusing finger, telling the world how bad it was. He came to help, to put the world right again. Anyone who trusts in him is acquitted; anyone who refuses to trust him has long since been under the death sentence without knowing it. And why? Because of that person's failure to believe in the one of-a-kind Son of God when introduced to him. [19-21] *"This is the crisis we're in: God-light streamed into the world, but men and women everywhere ran for the darkness. They went for the darkness because they were not really interested in pleasing God. Everyone who makes a practice of doing evil, addicted to denial and illusion, hates God-light and won't come near it, fearing a painful exposure. But anyone working and living in truth and reality welcomes God-light so the work can be seen for the God-work it is."*

Many of us have experienced all types of betrayal. For example, in our homes amongst our parents and children, on our jobs, in our marriages, in the church, or literally anywhere we have allowed our feet to walk. We can choose to accept the betrayal as something strange that has come upon us to destroy us or as something that has come our way and is giving us an opportunity to grow and prosper.

Being on top of the world and having it all together feels great, but having everything go as planned and not having to deal with any issues in life can make us complacent and unappreciative at times. It is our typical nature, even as Christians, to just go through the motion and wait on the rapture; if there is such a thing. It's in our human nature to just do what seems good and be satisfied with the results.

Every once in a while, our boat needs to be rocked and we need to fall into the water head first unaware of what is in the water. We need to trust that God is essential as we fall into an unknown area. This is when He can get our attention the best. Dealing with betrayal can sometimes cause us to sing "oh my, oh my" or "why me Lord," but sometimes God is asking why not you?

In our effort to overcome betrayal, it is best to come to some realizations in our faith or in our NO faith (fear); that our faith needs to be tested. When we go through a test, we ask questions such as; what am I going to do? How am I going to handle this situation or who am I going to lean on? Tests, trials, and storms are not only necessary for us, but they become a testimony to unbelievers that our God is real.

Unbelievers are those who have no faith in God; they need to be drawn by the miracle working power of God, and experience his love just as those of us who were in sin before we became Christians. There are many examples of Gods power throughout the bible that will build faith in unbelievers but they may never read or understand the Bible.

We as believers should be walking Bibles and show the world who our God is! We can't do this by mumbling and complaining every time we experience a storm.

The miracles Jesus performed showed unbelievers that anything is possible with Christ. He demonstrated his power to unbelievers by the working of miracles. Even we as Saints need to be reminded from time to time that God is still real and in control; but faith says, if He doesn't do it, HE is still a God who is able **(Daniel 3: 16-18)**. We need to have a relationship with Him while teaching others to do the same. Remember, no matter what the test, we should never allow our faith to dwindle.

That the trial of your faith, being much more precious than of gold that perishes, though it be tried

with fire, might be found unto praise and honor and
glory at the appearing of Jesus Christ:

1 Peter 1:7 (KJV)

[2]Consider it nothing but joy, my brothers and
sisters, whenever you fall into various trials. [3]Be
assured that the testing of your faith [through
experience] produces endurance [leading to
spiritual maturity, and inner peace]. [4] And let
endurance have its perfect result and do a thorough
work, so that you may be perfect and completely
developed [in your faith], lacking in nothing.
James 1:2-4 (AMP)

Oftentimes, sin makes us feel unworthy to experience an all-powerful, miraculous God. So, when we meet others who do not know him; we sell them a false hokiest God who seems to be unrealistic because our lives are not real; that's hypocrisy or religion with no power or relationship. When I was an unbeliever, I searched for real genuine people who understood my struggles and were willing to show me a way of deliverance.

Whether you are an unbeliever or a new convert who is immature in your faith, it is important to understand that life is full of trials, struggles, and disappointments, BUT you are an overcomer by the blood of the lamb and by the words of your testimony.

I am reminded of a time when I thought I was going to lose our son. It was around February of 1994 when our son, Christopher, was riding a bicycle without a helmet, in disobedience. At the time he was about 7 years old and we had just moved into our new home. We were happy and thought nothing could go wrong. God had blessed us to buy a nice three-bedroom home while still in bankruptcy. While being obedient and trusting Him, God enabled us to buy a house for less than what we paid for our first SUV. God had made it possible for us to move out of a neighborhood where fights and shootings took place, just outside of our home, every weekend. I hated our old neighborhood and was grateful when God opened the door for us to move; but back to my testimony about my son...

Christopher got onto a bicycle that belonged to my nephew; he had ridden it to our new home as he volunteered to help carry some things into the house. The bicycle was too big for Christopher and I had previously told him that I didn't have time to search for his helmet. I was extremely proud of our first home and was very eager to move in, so I began moving what I could while my husband; Joey was at work. I did not desire to spend another night in the old house.

I had been a follower of Jesus Christ for about two years and it had been very difficult as the only Christian in our home; the flesh warred against the spirit daily. God blessing us with our own home showed that He honored my hearts' desire; this was truly a breakthrough and a tremendous blessing.

In the process of moving, I went to pick up other items for the house; leaving Christopher and his two sisters with my aunt Geneva.

When I left, undoubtedly, Christopher got back on the bicycle. I arrived back in our new neighborhood shortly thereafter and saw Christopher on the bicycle trying to get home before I could see him. In an effort to dodge me, he took another route, thinking I didn't see him. I did not deal with Christopher's disobedience right away and, because I was trying to get things done before it got dark, began removing things from the car taking them into the house.

As I walked down the hallway, I heard the worse scream of my life. It was my aunt Geneva who remained outside watching the girls. I immediately knew that something was seriously wrong so I rushed outside and there was Christopher lying unconscious in the middle of the street. I panicked picking him up, not thinking about his injuries, but wanting to get him out of the street and to the hospital.

We lived one block from the hospital, however, at the time I could not find my way too it. I was looking at it but I could not cause my car to turn in that direction until I audibly spoke, telling myself to go in the direction of the hospital. I walked into the hospital and tried to speak but nothing would come out of my mouth.

I recall a Caucasian woman sitting in the waiting area reading a magazine; she spoke on my behalf to a nurse who was very rude. The woman told the nurse to help me with my son. When Christopher was released to the doctors, I went back to the registration area to fill out paperwork and to thank that white-headed Caucasian lady but the nurse told me that there was no one in front of me waiting to be seen. She treated me as though I had lost my mind, but I knew I was not going crazy and was sure of what I had seen. In case you are wondering I believe it was an angel.

We were informed that Chris was suffering from major head trauma which was affecting his heart rate; it was decreasing by the minute. The emergency room doctor told me that I needed to prepare for the worse because he did not believe he was going to make it; but my faith kicked in! I discovered faith I didn't know I had. I begged God not to take our only son away from us; not realizing at the time that I didn't have to beg but simply ask and believe in His word.

During this time, I was a spiritual infant in my Christian walk and didn't understand my place in the Lord.

My heart cried out to God, the Holy Spirit took over, and I was consumed with his glory as a heavenly language, I knew nothing about, came forth. The Lord wrapped His loving arms around me and assured me that Christopher was going to be okay. While I was praying a nurse told me that she thought I had gone into shock and needed to call someone to be with me, so I called my dad and my husband who, at the time, worked about 20 miles away.

I prayed to God for my son to get the proper treatment he needed immediately! When I looked through the emergency room window and saw my lifeless little boy lying on the table, I became very angry. The doctor seemed to have given up on our son, as he and what appeared to be medical students, simply walking around him not knowing what to do," BUT

GOD!"

A doctor who had been called in for another patient intervened after a part-time nurse, who was also Christopher's second grade teacher at the time, whispered into his ear about what was going on. That doctor immediately stopped what he was doing and demanded that an ambulance come and take Christopher to another city to be treated for his head injury. Christopher was transported to Macon, Georgia where he underwent several tests. We waited for hours.

I waited with assurance that God was going to heal him but my husband, who was very upset, paced the floor constantly. After tests were completed, the doctor reported that there was no blood on Christopher's brain and admitted him in the intensive care unit. He had all types of machines hooked up to him.

In addition to my concern for Christopher's condition, I was fearful because we had to deal with a social worker who came in hour after hour asking if I had harmed my son. I repeatedly told her the same story and after several hours of being interrogated by her, the Holy Spirit took over. After about the fourth time I was filled with boldness and refused to answer any more questions.

I sat staring at the social worker as I worried about my son. She finally concluded that she could see that there was no way that I could have hurt him so she left. I read the bible to Christopher every day and fasted by his bedside. I was criticized by family members for doing so, but I knew what God had promised. I knew he would live a quality life and not be a vegetable; as the doctor in Warner Robins had informed me.

God told me that Christopher would be just fine and that he was going to heal him completely, so I read the bible to him and waited. At the time, I recognized it both as a test of my faith and a means of drawing my husband to have faith in an almighty God.

Chris was unconscious for three days and on that third day, literally around noon, he opened his eyes. The first doctor stated that if he gained consciousness, we would have to take care of a disabled child for the rest of his life. While praying to God I asked for total healing, reminded Him that he doesn't half do anything, and asked that He please keep His promise. God healed Chris completely! He had some struggles for about two years but after that he was able to play baseball, football and basketball with no problems.

Chris became a musician in the school band and, for several years, played drums for our local church. To this day, he is still an awesome musician. My faith was tested, and my husband who, at the time did not believe, experienced God in a miraculous way; he began to believe. After that experience, I believed God could do anything and was assured that it was all a test to show both me and Joey just how powerful God is.

Sometimes we are like Thomas, in the Bible; he had to actually see for himself **(John 20:25-27)**. Occasionally, we need to see God's miracle working power in our lives before we truly believe He is God. The spirit of Thomas, is to have little faith. It is okay at times because it gives opportunity for God to show up and show out in our lives. Sometimes He blows our minds!

Because God has done so many miraculous things in my life, I recognize that He is able and will always believe Him for miracles! Our marriage is a miracle! Our redeemed adult children (by faith) are miracles! My own life, as I have experienced many near death experiences, is a miracle!

Immediately following the accident involving our son, I was overwhelmed with fear. The thought of being betrayed and losing something or someone extremely valuable to you will bring fear. At the time I didn't know how important it was to know the Bible, as I know it today. I am learning more each and every day. By studying the Word and listening to chosen spiritual leaders, I learned that we must fight in the spiritual realm against the rulers of darkness.

There are forces of satan, the enemy, who desire to kill, steal, and destroy our children, grandchildren, nieces, nephews, family, friends, and those whose God has ordained with purpose and destiny. We must remember that Jesus came to give us life and that more abundantly **(John10:10)**. We must be in position, spiritually, to pray and intercede if we are to break the chains of bondage and yoke of sin from the lives of sinners. We must be in position to assist in love.

Not everyone is fortunate enough to experience the miracle we encountered with our son. Months later we saw reports that a little girl, who had experienced the same type of accident while wearing a helmet, but became paralyzed from her neck down. We learned that she was wearing a helmet during her accident;

which made things that much more fascinating about God.

Chris wasn't wearing any physical protection... BUT THANK THE LORD FOR HIS SUPERNATURAL PROTECTION! God is so good to His people; all we have to do is trust in Him and not ourselves.

Even if Christopher had experienced such disability, God would still have had a purpose and a plan for his life; just as I believe he had for the little girl who was paralyzed as a result of her accident. We should always remember that it is not over until God says it is over. God may have healed her completely later in life but if He didn't, we know He is still able.

God is continually molding us as we surrender to Him daily. If we allow Him, He guides and instructs us. It is when we fail to acknowledge Him in all our ways and allow Him to direct our paths that we find ourselves in unnecessary trouble **(Proverbs 3:5-6)**. I am so thankful that he is a merciful and forgiving God who will NEVER leave me or forsake me **(Deuteronomy 31:6, 8)** even when I did some of the most stupid things.

We experience betrayal when we place our trust in flesh and blood rather than in God. The flesh can never dwell in the presence of God because it cannot relate to Him. . . He is spirit.

In **John 4:23-24** the bible says that we are to worship God in spirit and in truth. Individuals who betray others and operate in lies and deceit have an evil spirit and are influenced by Satan. God made mankind in His image and in His likeness, as stated in **Genesis 1:27**. In **Jeremiah 1: 4-7;** God talks about knowing Jeremiah before he was in his mother's womb; so, if God knew Jeremiah, He also knew us before we were born.

Oftentimes individuals don't know they are operating with the rulers of darkness. One thing I have learned about darkness is that if someone strikes or shoots in a dark place, anyone is liable of getting hit or attacked. Spiritually speaking, everyone is lost and in darkness until the spirit of Light-Jesus, is allowed to rule in them. Darkness comes against light and, since the two are different, it does not comprehend it.

People who are in darkness, or lost in sin don't understand people who have been redeemed and brought into God's marvelous light. Those of us who have been redeemed from darkness and have the Spirit of God living in us, have a responsibility to bring others into the light and to help them to see that light

(Mathew 5:14). Turning on a light in a dark room always defeats the darkness, even if it is through the use of a flashlight.

Light exposes the enemy and gives way for him, along with those who operate with him, to be destroyed. We must be mindful of our actions and choose not to indulge in the lust of the flesh; that includes gossip, backbiting, defaming, and murdering others with our tongue. If you know anything about gardening, you know that whatever is planted or sown, is also harvested or reaped. We also understand that our harvest may be good or bad and may return in an abundance; whether an abundance of blessings or an abundance of curses.

We need to watch what we put into the atmosphere as we are judged by every idle word **(Mathew 12:36).** Think about times when you have spoken something to someone, whether good or bad, and it seemed to multiply or grow into something bigger. The Bible tells us that we have what we say, in addition, we have what we think. If we think and say that we are a failure that is what we will be, but if we speak those things that are not as though they are like our Father did **(Romans 4:17)**; we can experience God's miraculous power to change any situation in our lives. **Ephesians 5:12** tells us that it is shameful even to speak of those things which are done by them in secret.

⁶And the tongue is a fire. [The tongue is a] world of wickedness set among our members, contaminating and depraving the whole body and setting on fire the wheel of birth (the cycle of man's nature), being itself ignited by hell. ⁷For every kind of beast and bird, of reptile and sea animal, can be tamed and has been tamed by human genius (nature). ⁸But the human tongue can be tamed by no man. It is a restless (undisciplined, irreconcilable) evil, full of deadly poison. ⁹with it we bless the Lord and Father, and with it we curse men who were made in God's likeness! ¹⁰Out of the same mouth come forth blessing and cursing. These things, my brethren, ought not to be so.

James 3:6-10 (Amplified Bible)

⊘ CHAPTER THREE ⊘

Betrayal in the Nest

Betrayal is nothing new to Christians. The bible tells us about betrayal and all sorts of other problems associated with life. Betrayal started way back with the first family, Adam and Eve, while in the Garden of Eden with the serpent.

God gave Adam and Eve eternal life but in choosing to be disobedient, they chose death. The serpent fooled Eve who then persuaded her husband to follow the enemy's ways. After Adam and Eve disobeyed God, in Genesis 3, the earth was introduced to betrayal and evil-sinful wickedness, discomfort, sorrow, and distress invaded the earth.

Cain and Abel are another example of betrayal, they were the offspring of Adam and Eve and are examples of a generational curse within the same nest. In **Genesis 4** God favored Abel because he presented his best offering from the fruit of his labor. Cain, on the other hand, most likely presented his offering out of obligation, giving God "a portion," which was essentially stealing and withholding from God, so his sacrifice was not honored.

Cain was not as blessed as Abel because of the way he chose to give. He presented his offering with a nasty attitude and a filthy heart. Abel, as a result of his offering, was promoted and exalted. This made Cain angry so he killed his own flesh and blood; his brother.

I am reminded of **Matthew 6:19-21, 33**, where the bible teaches us to not store up our treasures here on earth where they can be stolen, but to store them in heaven where no one can steal them because wherever our treasure is there is where our heart is also.

I believe Cain worshipped the earth, which is a symbol of the flesh, more instead of treasuring what really matters, giving God a pure sacrifice. How many of us give God any old thing and expect Him to bless it? Jesus is asking for more, as a matter of fact, He wants all of us. I must admit, I have struggled in this area, but in times when I have totally surrendered my all to Him, "OH MY GOD!" He has shown Himself mightily in my life! He wants all of us and not just part of us.

He is no different than we are in this area; when we have someone special in our life, such as our spouse, we want all of them and are not willing to share them with another. God only honors marriage between two people of the opposite sex, a male and a female. There is never a time when we should be willing to share our spouse with another.

If our heart is continuously on our job, possessions, and other tangible things, we leave no room for God. Serving tangible things will never give us complete satisfaction; we can only get that from the one who made us. When we are dissatisfied, we tend to feel hurt and betrayed as Cain did. As a result, our actions can become extreme and place us outside of the will of God.

Mathew 6:33 teaches us to seek first the Kingdom of Heaven and God's righteousness and all things we desire will be added unto us. When we seek the Kingdom of Heaven, we only desire heavenly things and those things that God has promised us. Our hearts are not filled with greed and covetousness, because we recognize it to be sin. As we set our desire upon God and seek Him and we desire to live lives that are pleasing to Him, rather than live in sin.

Psalms 37:4 tells us to, "delight ourselves in the Lord and He will give us the desires of our hearts." Merriam Webster defines delight as, "a means of taking pleasure in another." Our walk with God should be a walk of pleasure and satisfaction but, unfortunately, some of us view it as if it is a duty to serve Him. God made all things for us to enjoy but we often allow "things" to take our attention away from God **(1 Timothy 6:17)**. Things were not meant to replace God in our lives.

Abel took pleasure in serving God as he brought God his best. He didn't give God his leftovers. As a result, he was favored over his brother Cain. **Malachi 3:10** teaches us to bring all the tithe into the storehouse-an abundant supply of provision for the saints that there may be enough meat or provision for everyone; (natural and spiritual). A tithe is simply ten percent of one's earnings.

In **Malachi 3:6-9,** God explains how He expects for us to follow the decrees concerning tithe and offerings. He also tells us how man will refuse his decrees (official order issued by a legal authority) which would result in a curse; even amongst nations. God states that man will rob Him in tithe and in offerings.

We may not understand how Abel was blessed because he was murdered by his brother Cain **(Genesis 4)**. Abel's flesh was dead but his spirit lived for eternity; unlike Cain who was cursed for killing him. Although Cain betrayed God, his brother and his parents; God had great mercy for Cain and extended divine grace to him. Even after cursing Cain; God allowed him to live and dared anyone to bother him.

Cain did not heed God's instruction but allowed evil to take over. He had the opportunity to do what was right but, like many of us, he allowed pride to get the best of him and acted out of the wrong motive. It is amazing how many times we feel betrayed by others but "the proof is in the pudding," betrayal often comes when we ourselves step out of the will of God for our lives.

Spouses tend to blame one another when the marriage is lacking, when it is oftentimes a result of not investing adequate time with one another, due to a lack of communication, or not placing value on one another. We blame others when our children are wayward and get into drugs, join gangs, or become parents out of wedlock, when it was us who stopped or never instilled the values of **(Proverbs 22:6)** in them.

Sometimes we feel betrayed when we are not successful but, if we really consider, it was us who failed to put forth the effort and obtain more skills, advance our education, or explore the gifts God placed within us. Sometimes we think we've been betrayed in our local church because we feel that the man or woman of God is not giving us enough spiritual substance to sustain us when it is our responsibility to study and apply ourselves to knowing God's Word.

Light Bearers

[12] Therefore, my beloved, as you have always obeyed, not as in my presence only, but now much more in my absence, work out your own salvation with fear and trembling; *[13] for it is God who works in you both to will and to do for His good pleasure. [14] Do all things without complaining and disputing, [15] that you may become blameless and harmless, children of God without fault in the midst of a crooked and perverse generation, among whom you shine as lights in the world, [16] holding fast the word of life, so that I may rejoice in the day of Christ that I have not run in vain or labored in vain.*

Philippians 2:12-16 (NKJV)

2Timothy 2:15, 20-21 is another example of us taking responsibility for our own soul. *[15] Be diligent to present yourself approved to God, a worker who does not need to be ashamed, rightly dividing the word of truth.[20] But in a great house there are not only vessels of gold and silver, but also of wood and clay, some for honor and some for dishonor. [21] Therefore if anyone* *cleanses himself from the latter, he will be a vessel for honor, sanctified and useful for the Master, prepared for every good work.*

When we stand before Jesus, we will have no excuse. **2Timothy 2:20-21** teaches us about vessels of honor and dishonor. We are to cleanse ourselves in order to be sanctified for the Master's use that we may be prepared for every good work. We all have an individual journey to walk out, which includes fasting, praying, and seeking God. As individuals, we are responsible for learning God's Word and allowing the Holy Spirit to lead us into truth. We are responsible for rejecting the lies of Satan, our enemy.

Betrayal within the home is difficult to overcome, but with Jesus, all things are possible; He is our strength. I am reminded of the devastating crisis which took place in our home. The act of infidelity and birthing a child outside of our marriage. The devil meant it for evil but I trusted in Jesus, all things will work together for our good. God is a forgiving Father, even when people are not so forgiving. He blesses us in the midst of life's storms; our trials and tribulations. Every person does dumb stuff at some point in time, some of us just do dumber things; perhaps because of ignorance, fear, peer pressure or sinful desires.

Regardless of what you have done, know that God is a restorer, rebuilder, and a replenisher. He will give you another chance if you put your trust in Him; I am a living testimony of that!

Our homes should be a place of love, peace, trust and freedom. A place where we can relax and let our guards down. We should be comfortable disclosing our weaknesses and humiliations when around family. We should be able to interact without walls, fear of bondage resulting from judgment, betrayal, or mistrust. Parents have a responsibility to ensure their children are secure and safe in their home. Children have a responsibility to respect and honor their parents by showing their obedience **(Ephesians 6:1)**.

Betrayal in the nest often occurs when trust and respect is broken. Most families can continue to love one another no matter what, but love must be accompanied by respect and trust so that divine healing can take place. My family is a living testimony. It took the supernatural power of God to straighten the mess created in our home as a result of sin. Parents with unresolved issues create children with bigger issues in all facets of life and throughout society.

Generational curses are established and compounded when issues are not dealt with. For example, when parents use drugs such as marijuana, cocaine, or pills and are not delivered, their children often choose to use more dangerous drugs such as meth or heroin.

Parents who were promiscuous, or committed sexual sins without being delivered often pass those spirits on to their children and the sinful acts multiply. Their children proceed to have several sexual relations out of wedlock, oftentimes with several different partners. The results can lead to contracting deadly diseases.

As parents, we should be very careful about what we share with our children concerning our past, because children are strongly pressured by their peers to try anything. Households are always under attack by the enemy, because Satan realizes that if he can destroy the family unit, then he can destroy a church, a community, a school, a state and a nation similar to Eli's sons in *1 Samuel 12-34.*

Eli's sons, Hophni and Phinehas, had no respect for God and, although Eli was a man of God, he allowed his evil sons to continue taking possessions from the Israelites and sleeping with their women. Eli had to have felt hurt and betrayed as a man of God. He failed to correct his sons for whatever reason so God sent a man of God to ask Eli why his sons were more important than He.

Eli's sons were fattened as they ate the choice parts of every offering made by the Israelites as sacrifices to God. The messenger warned Eli that God declared He would cut Eli's strength as well as his father's strength and that there would be no old man in his lineage. He also stated that his sons would die on that same day. God's promise to Eli came to pass in **1 Samuel 4:12-22.** The actions of Eli and his sons caused the glory of the Lord to leave their lives. The wife of Phinehas was pregnant when her husband was killed, and this caused her to go into labor.

Eli's daughter-in-law named the baby Ichabod; meaning that the glory of the Lord had departed from Israel. God's glory had departed from an entire nation, giving way for the enemy to take possession of the ark of God. Due to their evil ways, the Philistines could not keep the ark in their possession either so they took it to Gath, and while moving it from place to place, God continued to pass judgment, just as He had in Eli's house.

Eli's disobedience was passed down to his sons who became not only disobedient but rebellious and shameful in the sight of God and an entire nation.

Unfortunately, Eli is not the only father who refused to get his house in order and follow the will of God. Fathers who are supposed to be the head of their homes; they are charged by God to lead their families in a Godly way. Due to his lack of leadership, David also had issues in his home. Perhaps God passed judgment on David's household as a consequence of him lying with Bathsheba; another man's wife.

David's household experienced a lot of betrayal within the nest. Some of us know David as a king who was slacking off when he should have been at war. In the mist of David slacking off, he noticed the wife of another man taking a bath. He desired her so much so that he eventually had her husband killed **(2 Samuel Chapter 11).** We see David as a murderer and an adulterer, but God knew and looked at David's heart. His heart was sincere toward God, but God did not ignore David's actions. At the result of his sin with Bathsheba, their first-born son died at birth and great turmoil surfaced in his home amongst his other children as we find in **(2 Samuel 12).**

Betrayal that surfaces in a Christian home happens when the enemy trespasses and enters as a thief and a robber. It is often because someone was sleeping (not on post) or left the door open. It is Satan's goal to hinder our godly reproduction and if we don't wake up in time our entire family can become a casualty.

Betrayal as we learned with Cain and Abel was disastrous, but the type of betrayal David experienced was something one may have never expected; especially because of who he was.

In **2 Samuel 13** the bible explains how Amnon the brother of Tamar pretended to be sick to get her sympathy because, deep in his heart, he desired to lay with her. Tamar being a good sister fell into the trap of lust and violence as she attempted to serve her brother Amnon at his house. She was trying to make him feel better. . . or so she thought. When Tamar got close enough to Amnon, he grabbed her, pulled her into his bed, raped her, and in the act, filled her with anguish and grief. When David discovered the rape, it angered him a great deal as Amnon had brought tremendous shame to the family; after all David was the king.

The act of betrayal caused several people to be hurt and full of sorrow especially after Amnon turned the table and blamed Tamar for her own rape. At that point he had grown to hate her. Amnon's reaction is not too different from many reactions today, as rape victims are often blamed for being at the wrong place at the wrong time, or with the wrong people.

Amnon committed a very selfish act that caused discord and evil to rise up within his family. His brother Absalom desired his throat and unfortunately kills Amnon, causing much more grief to the family. King David, a mighty warrior and leader in the sight of man, was favored by God to lead several battles, but could not conquer the battles in his own nest.

David and Bathsheba had a past; one that caused the death of their first-born son and possibly passed down the rage, selfishness, and violent spirit to his own sons as he had Uriah killed for no apparent reason, other than to take his wife.

Oftentimes generational curses linger and travel through the bloodline if they are not broken. This may have been the case in David's house. After David committed his act with Bathsheba, Amnon took his sisters' innocence, then Absalom murdered his own brother.

Most godly parents invest all that they can into their children by training them to be holy and imparting good moral character into them, but sometimes the unthinkable happens. Instead of losing hope; we should watch and pray for answers and discern who is in control of our children's spirit, especially when we have examined ourselves and concluded that the problem did not originate with us.

The Bible gives simple instructions on how we are to conduct ourselves as a family **(Ephesians 6:1-4).** Our children are very precious to God and, with the supernatural power that comes when we pray and fast, we must break the curse of rebellion, disobedience, and all demonic influence off their lives at an early age.

I am reminded of a testimony that a cousin shared after her aunt who raised her from a young child passed away and went on to be with Jesus. My cousin spoke at the home going celebration and shared how she never saw her aunt complain or give up on God; even in the mist of pain and suffering; while battling cancer, dealing with an unfaithful husband, and the pain of a divorce.

I remember visiting Aunt Mary after school on several occasions while I was in high school. She was pleasant to be around and imparted so much love and wisdom into my life. I remember the unconditional love she shared for a niece who was my cousin; she had two children, and although living in a sinful state, Aunt Mary allowed them to live with her. Aunt Mary treated her like a daughter and never gave up on her. Today my cousin is a Christian, is married to a wonderful

Christian man, and is a very successful teacher with the same loving spirit as Aunt Mary. My cousin is a living witness that a curse can be broken and a life can be restored to victory.

We do not have to live under the curse of sin, regardless of what we have done in the past. Jesus became a curse for us that we may be freed from bondages, redeemed, and walking in the promises of Abraham by his spirit; therefore, we do not have to pass these things down to other generations **(Galatians 3:13 -14)**. Through the blood of Jesus, we can be free from sin and death, and be a blessing in the earth for those who don't believe.

In 2 Corinthians 5:17, the Bible teaches us that if anyone be in Christ; walking in his statutes, standards, and according to his commandments, he is a new creation; old things are passed away and we become new. Denounce the curse and walk in a blessed hope that Jesus Christ can only give. He is waiting for us to choose to walk in the newness of life **(Romans 6:4)**.

John 10:10 says that the enemy comes to steal, kill, and destroy. The enemy is after our families who often deal with so many life issues; but we must come to understand that Jesus came so we could have life and that more abundantly. God is able to do exceeding, abundantly more than we can ask or think **(Ephesians 3:20)**. Don't give any place in your home, marriage, or relationships to the devil because the devil seeks vessels to dwell in (inhabit) just as God does.

The enemy knows that if he can plant the spirit of betrayal in a marriage it is destined to fail, "But God". The vows made during a marriage are serious but, for some reason, some of us don't take them to heart. Perhaps we were too young to understand or on "cloud nine" with our head stuck in the clouds and not really listening to the seriousness of the commitment.

Maybe we allowed outside influences to interfere with the commitment of being married to our spouse. Outside influences such as our parents, friends, or family members. Unfortunately, many marriages are influenced by the desire to connect with an individual in the flesh; while love and commitment is not the main focus. Some couples who become engaged focus too much on the fantasy of a wedding and completing the ceremony so the honeymoon can start.

Based on data I found on the "Focus on the Family" website; divorce rate among Christians is significantly lower than the general population. Many people who seriously practice a traditional religious faith such as Christianity, have a divorce rate marked lower than the general population. The factor making the most difference is religious commitment and practice. Couples who regularly practice any combination of serious religious behaviors and attitudes such as: attending church together, studying their Bibles, and praying privately with one another are less likely to choose divorce.

Professor Bradley Wright, a sociologist at the University of Connecticut, explains from his analysis of people who identify as Christians but rarely attend church, that 60 percent have been divorced. Of those who attend church regularly, 38 percent have been divorced.

The divorce rates of believers are not identical to the general population. Being a committed, faithful believer makes a measurable difference in marriage. Saying you believe something or merely belonging to a church, unsurprisingly, does little for marriage.

The more a couple actually becomes involved in the actual practice of their faith by learning the word of God and fellowshipping with those who do the same, the greater impact this has in strengthening both the quality and longevity of a marriage. Faith does matter and the leading sociologists of family and religion confirm this (Stanton 2011).

Marriage is more than a honeymoon; it is a lifelong commitment between a man and a woman. Sometimes we can marry the wrong person and not realize it until after some time has gone by. We look at our situation and question what we have gotten ourselves into. After maturity sets in, we often fail to correct things by allowing God to do the work He needs to do in our lives. He teaches us to love unconditionally, but unfortunately, selfishness and betrayal are manifested. We failed to realized that the first act of betrayal was made the moment we said "I Do" when in actuality, we should have said "I can't or I shouldn't."

The worse betrayal in a marriage is going through the motions while having no interest in the other individual; until something is needed such as money or sex. Money and sex are good but should not be used as a pawn; not at the price of being unhappy or miserable.

Our marriage has been through many storms and we have stayed for reasons other than true love at times, but when we allowed the love of Jesus to flood our hearts, we no longer stayed out of obligations, but because of true love. True relationships are built on love, patience, commitment, and communication, by both individuals.

1 Corinthians 13 describes the type of love commitment we should have for one another. Before committing to what should be lifelong relationships; wise counsel, communication, and commitment are necessary. We should seek these things before saying, "I Do".

Men and women can bring so much baggage to a marriage, and it is oftentimes necessary to identify the baggage so it can be dealt with; especially if there are children involved and when there is blending of families. It is so important to set goals and come to an agreement on how to achieve those goals before committing to someone who doesn't believe in you and is not in your corner.

Before getting married, goals and dreams need to be brought to the table so that once a couple is united into Holy Matrimony, they are on the same page rather than going in two different directions. Obtaining counseling from a reliable, godly, and neutral source is great for a marriage, especially if one doesn't have a good understanding of what marriage is about. Some of us come from divorced families, abusive homes, or single parent homes where we never saw examples of a true loving marriage; or perhaps we saw marriages filled with manipulation and selfishness.

The Bible is the best teacher on anything we may experience in life, including how a marriage is supposed to be. Instructions are found in **1 Corinthians 7:1-6, 9-11; Ephesians 5:22-33; and Matthew 5:30-32.** In **Genesis 2:24,** the bible tells us that a man should leave his father and mother and cleave-to (adhere, or bind himself to) his wife and they (husband and wife) shall become one flesh. They should possess loyalty and an unwavering commitment towards one another.

I've always wondered how two individuals can become one flesh. God gave me this analogy while walking on the beach one day, enjoying His beautiful ocean. One flesh is just that, oneness in spirit, and even in the natural. For example, if I walk into a room of friends or associates, they should know who I am married to.

My last name is not Johnson, Jones, or Williams so they should recognize that I am Mrs. Bishop without reservation. Sometimes we get things twisted both on our jobs and in the church. Some men outside of the home and in other arenas, get confused when women do not submit to them as a wife submits to her husband. On my job, I am not a wife; I am an employee, a co-worker, or a supervisor, and although of the opposite sex, I should have the same rights, support, and benefits as anyone, including my male counterparts Some of you need to seek God and learn how to differentiate your role as a spouse and an employee, coworker, etc. It is important to learn how you are to conduct yourself and how you should be treated when you are working in your career field or profession. Your value and importance are no different than anyone else.

Ephesians 5 tells us how Jesus views at us as His bride. We are to be without spot or blemish just as He is. He is our husbandman and the world should be able to see that our name has changed from sinner to saint, as we display His image and His likeness. Godly husbands and wives should display the life of Christ as (one) with Him. We should be only one flesh in marriage and serve Christ Jesus, in mind, body, soul, and spirit.

"Wives submit to their own husbands as to the Lord. Husbands are the head of the wife as Christ is the head of the church and he is the savior of the body. As the church is subject unto Christ, so let the wives be to their own husbands in everything. Husbands, love your wives even as Christ loved the church and gave himself for it that he might sanctify and cleanse it with the washing of water by the word; that he might present it to himself a glorious church,

not having spot or wrinkle but that it should be holy and without blemish; so ought men to love their wives as their own bodies and he that loves his wife loves himself. No man hate's his own flesh but nourishes and cherishes it even as the Lord does the church. We are members of Jesus body and of his flesh and of his bones. For this cause shall a man leave his father and mother and shall be joined unto his wife and the two shall be one flesh.

Ephesians 5:22-33 (KJV)

If I am bone of my husband's bone and flesh of his flesh, as Adam declared Eve was, then Eve should be the image of Adam as well as God. We all know that Adam was put to sleep and a God took a rib from his side, not a back bone or a foot bone, but from his side. God used it to form Eve; a helper for Adam (**Genesis 2:2123).** God gave Adam a woman to help him; not to control or manipulate him into doing things he shouldn't do. This is one-way betrayal can surface or take place in a marriage.

Genesis 2:25 teaches that Adam and Eve were both naked and unashamed; they had nothing to hide. God has a way of bringing the truth out of those who truly submit and surrender to Him. Satan keeps secrets, hides things, and uses them to destroy individuals. This is not how God operates. Keeping secrets and hiding things from your spouse is act of betrayal and the enemy will later play mind games and attempt to use those things against each of you.

Of course; I am not referring to a surprise party or a gift, but secrets that cause trust issues and separation. If issues of betrayal are not dealt with according to the leading of the Holy Spirit, it can lead to great pain and seem almost impossible to restore; but God is able.

It is better to be open and honest from the beginning so that satan does not use our flaws as traps to cause suffering to or ruin our marriage relationships. Honesty truly is the best policy, even if it hurts. **John 8:32** teaches that we, "shall know the truth and the truth shall make us free." Let us endeavor to be truthful, at all costs, knowing that our Father in Heaven will always back us up.

Telling the truth while knowing it may hurt someone can be a frightening thing, but we must be led by the Holy Spirit in doing so. God's grace is sufficient to make the wrong become right in our relationships as we follow truth in Jesus.

Releasing sin from the soul and spirit, while embracing truth is a form of cleansing. Not releasing oneself can cause disease, pain, and shame that the enemy will use against you as long as you allow him to. Free yourself today and put the past behind you; your best days are sure to come.

Unconditional love is a key factor in a marriage; we shouldn't love for physical things such as sex, money, houses or cars etc. We should love because we are one flesh put together by God. Our marriage relationship after our relationship with Jesus Christ should be one of our top priorities. Taking one another for granted can lead to betrayal, bitterness, unforgiveness, and ultimately divorce.

If you feel as though you are doing all of the work in the relationship; stop and do what God has designed, you to do as a husband or wife and pray for the other spouse. Remember who is in control – GOD IS. Take time to complement (give completeness or make whole) your spouse and understand that many of your spouses' weaknesses should be your strengths and vice versa.

Overall, know that it is God who makes us complete. Take one day at a time to cherish your mate and remember that it is the two of you; not the children, not the church, not the in-laws or friends; just the two of you at the end of the day. Don't live a lie when it comes to your marriage or anything else for that matter. This can cause so many people to get hurt; especially if children are a factor.

Set goals in your marriage and aim to become one in spirit – by serving the same God and choosing not to be unequally yoked **(2 Corinthians 6:14)**. Get to know one another by spending adequate time together. Times of romance, companionship, both verbal and physical communication, and by being committed to being there when the other really needs you is very important to the health and longevity of your marriage. Remain committed until death do you part.

Marriage Goals: Present and Future

_____

_____

_____

_____

_____

_____

_____

_____

_____

_____

_____

_____

_____

Marriage Goals: Present and Future
(continue)

_____

_____

_____

_____

_____

_____

_____

_____

_____

_____

_____

☙ CHAPTER FOUR ☙

Betrayal in the Church

In today's world, we see division all around us; divorce rates are sky rocketing; people turning against one another on their jobs, etc. Even our inner man is at times divided, causing us to be double minded and unstable; which can sometimes lead us to do the unthinkable.

Unfortunately, we find that many of our churches are divided due to discrimination, disagreements, selfishness, envy, jealousy, and strife; all those things that Jesus taught against. Some Christians say that we are a part of the body of Christ but many say one thing and live contrary to what the word of God says; that is betrayal within itself because unbelievers of Christ expect to see a difference in us as Christians.

The body of Christs' standards should be much higher and overall different from that of the world. I expect to be talked about, scandalized and mistreated in the world but not in the church, or at least, not as part of the body of Christ.

"Many will say unto Jesus that day, have we not prophesized in thy name, we visited the sick, we fed the hungry, we did this and that but Jesus will reply, "Depart from me, I never knew you" **(Mathew 7:22-24).**

Knowing Jesus, requires that we have an intimate relationship with Him. To have an intimate relationship with Jesus, we must walk in His image and His likeness; which is a simple lifestyle of holiness **(1 Peter 1:13-16).** The image or likeness of another is simply a replica of that individual.

When I became a Christian, years ago, I was very naïve, religious, and just plain ignorant when it came to knowing who I was laboring amongst. I believed all church-going people were compassionate, loving, and kind like Jesus. I thought everyone in the church would accept me for who I was, but man did I get a wake-up call.

I faithfully served, although I continued to encounter pain and disappointment. I experienced things very similar to what I had experienced in the world; while living in sin.

I came to realize that people were just people living at different levels of obedience; even in the church. The pain I suffered was often the result of misunderstanding, miscommunication, and gossip; which is a sin. . . ask Miriam, Moses' sister. Don't get the wrong impression and misinterpret what I am saying. I love all people, but when I became a Christian, I didn't realize that we as individuals are on different levels and have differing personalities.

The body of Christ is a mixture of both educated and uneducated people. There are those with many abilities and those with limited abilities. The Bible tells us that we all have different gifts according to the grace given unto us **(Romans 12:6-7)**. It is important for people of God to know their purpose in the Kingdom of God; not knowing can cause a catastrophe.

The church is full of gifted people who possess skills to operate in various areas; it is crucial for each of us to find out who we really are in Jesus Christ. Some of us are gifted in working with children, some work well with the ministry for men or women, some of us work well in electronics or media, while others excel at teaching or preaching God's word. One of the main issues we have in the body of Christ is that many don't know their place.

It is when we are out of place operating in areas we are not called to; that people are more prone to get hurt.

Church government is set in order, similar to that of a city government, but its policies and procedures come directly from God's governing laws and commandments, rather than from man. It can be very confusing to receive orders or instructions from numerous people, or heads; especially when someone is allowed to take charge of something and leads with a spirit of pride.

I worked as a Deputy Sheriff for many years, there we had a Sheriff, a Major, a Captain, and several Sergeants but I received my orders directly from my Sergeant. Sometimes my Major would ask me to do something; in cases like that it is important to understand rank. Although the Sheriff was not my direct supervisor; I still honored and respected him as the Sheriff. He was superior over the entire Sheriff's Office but he had supervisors as well.

If a Sergeant were to give me an order, due to my respect for order and rank, I will not tell him or her to wait until I talk to the Sheriff or Captain. God is not the author of confusion or disorder as He so clearly says in **1 Corinthians 14:33**.

One thing I don't understand about the body of **Christ** sometimes is that we often choose not to follow the set man or woman who God has placed us in covenant with. A covenant, according to Webster is, "a solemn and binding agreement; an agreement of promise between two or more parties." We break covenant too often, choosing to go our separate ways without God's blessings. This can be very dangerous for us. Now, of course if the head of the organization is crooked, corrupt, or abusive, that is another story. No one should follow individuals who continue to humiliate, abuse, or doesn't lead by example. Sometimes connections are destroyed and, for whatever reason, reconnection is not an option.

The body of Christ should be on one accord and operating in the same spirit. If the body of Christ is double-minded or divided, then it is unstable (**James 1:8)**. Being double-minded, is operating in the flesh, the flesh wars with the Holy Spirit.

The Bible gives the body of Christ simple instructions on how to love in **1 Corinthians 13**, and is a perfect example of the love that Jesus portrays. If we walk as Jesus walked and are sensitive to the Holy

Spirit, He will guide us in the direction, we are to take concerning any given matter.

Betrayal takes place in a church when people step outside of their grace and interfere with what God is doing in an individuals' life or within the ministry. If we don't understand a thing, we should ask God and trust that He will help us to understand. We need to seek His Word out on a matter. Reading God's word will help us grow and prosper spiritually so we are not ignorant of the enemies' devices.

As a young Christian, I learned that betrayal can happen anywhere. However, it doesn't have to exist amongst believers, if we commit to exercising the power that Jesus displayed as He lived life. Jesus experienced betrayal time after time, as a testimony to show us how to respond. As Christians, we must first develop a relationship with God to have successful relationships with others. God teaches us that our relationship with Him is not based on what others think about it. He speaks to us as individuals and instructs us on what He wants us to do within the body of Christ; this often includes other people. Both leaders and lay members should stand in obedience to the call of our Heavenly Father. We will stand before Him one day and He will judge everything we have done while on the earth.

The Bible speaks of many great leaders, common people, and even sinners who caught the vision of Jesus Christ and made a difference in the world around them. Leaders such as Moses; whom God used to save a nation. God only spoke to Moses about His plan, not his wife, children, or other leaders in Moses circle but Moses included Joshua and Caleb.

David is another example of this; he was a mighty man of war. When God commanded David to fight; he only spoke to David who involved others in the kingdom. Betrayal can affect our actions, especially when we do not live in obedience to God's commandments.

I love scriptures, but I particularly love what **James 2:20** says, "Faith without works is dead." We are told that if we do our part and live in obedience to God, and allow Him to guide us, that all things will work together for our good, just as it did for Abraham, Rahab, and many others.

I truly believe that most betrayal comes when we turn from God and run after our own desires, lusts, and greed. History has shown that sometimes people who say they are called by God, get caught in sin because of some form of lust or greed; this causes shame to the church. None of us are exempt from falling into sin and temptation. I believe everyone has been at fault for being disobedient and, at some point, that disobedience may have led to heart break and betrayal.

God may have instructed us to wait on marriage, a certain career, a larger house, or perhaps moving out of your parents' house, but because of disobedience, pride, and/or lust, the enemy got the best of us we went through unnecessary sufferings. That spouse may have turned out to be a wolf in sheep's clothing, or perhaps the big house became unaffordable, so we ended up working longer hours and spending less time with God. Similar to the prodigal son in **Luke 15:11-32**, moving out too soon has been known to cause homelessness, but pride often causes individuals to wander from place to place seeking refuge that doesn't exist.; but thank God for mercy.

Pride can have us stuck on a job we hate, and we feel it is unfortunate because we have invested so much time in it that it doesn't make sense to turn back. The good news is that God's grace and mercy lasts forever **(Psalm 103:17; 118:1)**. It's not too late to pray and make the necessary changes; God will help and bless us along the way; even after we have made bad decisions.

The bible states that even the king's heart is in the hand of the Lord and He can direct it wherever He pleases **(Proverbs 21:1)**. If God can direct a kings' heart then surely, He can direct the heart of a wayward child, boss, spouse etc.... The bottom-line is this: God is able to change any situation if we allow Him to. This is true even when we have created situations due to our own disobedience.

We must learn to humble ourselves and allow God to exalt us in due season; before making life changing decisions. When it is time to be exalted, elevated, or glorified by the Father, who is the only one who can truly give spiritual promotion, we should realize that blessings from Him adds no sorrow **(Proverbs 10:22)**.

The enemy is a thief and often brings tests and trials in an attempt to steal, kill and destroy **(John 10:10)**. But we must always remember who granted the exaltation and seek to resolve things in the spirit rather than in the flesh. Our power doesn't measure up without God, even Jesus knew this, as He gave the Father Jehovah all of the credit **(John 10:37-38).**

If we are experiencing sorrow, distress, regret, or grief, it is important that we examine ourselves to see if the exaltation came from God or man. It is possible to live an abundant and joyous life with God as the head. I remember talking with my father about the tricks of the enemy during my early years of Christianity. My father stated that the devil is always trying to sell wooden nickels; counterfeit blessings but God has the real thing. The devil is a liar, a cheat and a phony and the sad part about it is that some people worship him as their god.

All of us were born in sin and shaped in iniquity but there is a God in Heaven who gave His Only Son Jesus to die for our sins so that we can be reborn by the Holy Spirit who gives us eternal life. We should wait on our change to come and when it does, accept it with open arms without fear or doubting. Godly changes often come to change our defeated way of thinking and make us better by giving us the mind of Christ, but we must be willing to move at God's command; spiritually, physically, and emotionally.

In John 5:2-8, Jesus came upon a man who was lying near a pool of healing waters; he had not walked in 38 years and the waters were stirring right before his eyes; indicating a possible miracle in the water. Jesus asked the man why did he not get into the pool that had healed so many others and the man told Jesus that he had been pushed aside every time he attempted to get into the pool. Jesus healed the man out of compassion but it makes me wonder if the man would have made an effort to push his way to get into the pool. I believe he could have been healed much sooner.

Betrayal by sickness, disease, heartaches, resulting from past pain can be healed if we get into the stirred water of the Holy Ghost. The Bible teaches us to stir up the gift of God within ourselves. The Lord put something in each of us before we were born as He told Jeremiah, "I knew you before you were in your mother's womb." It is our own responsibility to get ourselves in the pathway of being blessed and set free. In case we don't have the strength, Jesus still makes house calls, He did so for many in the Bible and, will do the same for us. We can only get the proper rest, satisfaction, and fullness of joy, when we give our issues to Jesus, our Savior, and He releases us from them.

> 28 *Come to Me, all you who labor and are heavy laden,*
> *and I will give you rest.* 29 *Take My yoke upon you*
> *and learn from Me, for I am gentle and lowly in*
> *heart, and you will find rest for your souls.* 30 *For My*
> *yoke is easy and My burden is light."*
>
> **Matthew 11:28-30 (NKJV)**

In **Mark 5:25-29**, we find an example of the woman who suffered with bleeding for twelve years. She searched out doctors who were not able to heal her but when *she touched*; I repeat *she touched* the hem of Jesus' garment and was immediately made well or whole. She mixed her faith with action.

Being made whole after betrayal amongst a body of believers is truly up to us. No man has more power than Jesus; if someone says they do, they are false and, just as satan lifted himself above the knowledge of God, desiring to be God Jehovah; he will be destroyed forever **(Revelation 12:7-12; 20:7-10)**. Satan will never inherit the Kingdom of God nor experience God's magnificent love, glory, and power; he will soon be destroyed by his creator, God-Jehovah.

As Christians, we are to follow Jesus Christ. If you are submitted to spiritual authority and they are not following Jesus, it is time to leave from under that authority; unless God instructs to remain and pray for change and restoration.

God wants to heal us of the pain that betrayal has caused; even if it originated in the church. We must have a willing mind and allow God to show us ourselves and not always seek to blame others. I know that betrayal can come from others acting out of evil but God can turn that evil into something good. Just like the invalid man who had been lame for 38 years **(John 5:1-9)**, we often give up too soon. But because we mean so much to God, He will make a house call.

We should never experience betrayal as a result of our own measures and inconsistencies. We should never spend time fighting and scratching for what doesn't belong to us. God's will and timing is best. We need to recognize what God has for us and go after it in our season of grace and favor. He has made all of us unique and has given each one of us certain gifts and abilities that will glorify Him, but we must know what those are, and operate in them to reach our divine destiny. Many individuals reject the call of God because of the pressure to compete, the lack of support, fear of rejection, or because of fear of bondage.

The apostle Paul had a better excuse than we have; if there is one. **Acts 9:1-19**, shares that Paul was literally converted from Saul by force. Before Paul's conversion, he was misguided to destroy the Kingdom of God. God knocked him down and re-directed him and, as a result of that experience, he became a man passionate about God and declared the Word of God everywhere God sent him. The disciples were men of God who walked with Jesus. Each of them was afraid to allow Paul to mingle or be around them due to his past.

The changing of Paul's name from Saul also changed his identity, character, purpose, as well as his destiny. Paul had a Koinonia (Greek) experience. This means that he now had fellowship. He experienced a social exchange, and he could now communicate and participate with doing God's Kingdom work. God choosing Paul simply shows that he has no respect of person or favoritism. He can use anyone or anything for that matter.

We as saints of God must allow Him to rekindle our passion, when the enemy tramps upon it, and not use excuses as to why we are not doing God's will.

Passion is the fuel that ignites purpose in one's life and ministry. Jesus showed his passion on the cross after walking the earth. He fulfilled his destiny and is now seated at the right hand of the Father.

Passion is simply, "a state or capacity of being, acted on by external agents or forces; intense driving or overmastering feeling of conviction or desire of deep interest."

We must continue to serve God despite the betrayal we may experience amongst church members; whether you were taken advantage of, publicly humiliated, lied on, or so forth. Serving God is about serving Him. We are His workmanship and He calls us His own.

The Father desires to look down and see His image and his likeness in us; we are His sons and daughters. He doesn't see flesh; He is looking for Himself; His spirit. It is no different than when we are blessed to have offspring, we desire to see our teachings in our own children; this is a result of our relationship. As Christians, we are God's offspring through Jesus. We are to walk, talk, and act as if we are His; living in loving obedience to His Word.

Operate in our individual giftings will help save lives from hell; as we plant, water, and allow God to give the increase for maximum growth. Betrayal surfaces many times when we try to be someone that we were not predestined to be. All souls were created to give God glory and live according to His commandments. I understand the word of God when it says that the letter killeth, but the spirit giveth life. We must remember that every word was inspired by the Holy Spirit.

Leading the body of Christ is a great responsibility. **Mathew 23:11** says, "the greatest among us should be our servant." We should never become as the Scribes and Pharisees, who always desired to be served, often took advantage of people, and desired to be worshiped. There is only one God we should worship and His name is Jesus.

[1]Then spake Jesus to the multitude, and to his disciples, [2]Saying the scribes and the Pharisees sit in Moses' seat: [3]All therefore whatsoever they bid you observe, that observe and do; but do not ye after their works: for they say, and do not. [4]For they bind heavy burdens and grievous to be borne, and lay them on men's shoulders; but they themselves will

not move them with one of their fingers. ⁵But all their works they do for to be seen of men: they make broad their phylacteries, and enlarge the borders of their garments, ⁶And love the uppermost rooms at feasts, and the chief seats in the synagogues, ⁷And greetings in the markets, and to be called of men, Rabbi, Rabbi. ⁸But be not ye called Rabbi: for one is your Master, even Christ; and all ye are brethren. ⁹And call no man your father upon the earth: for one is your Father, which is in heaven. ¹⁰Neither be ye called masters: for one is your Master, even Christ. ¹¹But he that is greatest among you shall be your servant.

Matthew 23:1-11 (KJV)

Since God doesn't show favoritism all of us are able to be used by God the Holy Spirit to lead others out of darkness into the marvelous light of Jesus Christ. **Ephesians 4:11-13,** tells us that God gave gifts unto mankind; the fivefold ministry gifts. He gave Apostles, Prophets, Evangelists, Pastors, and Teachers to perfect the saints. Some of us are not in this category of gifting, but He did not leave us out as he gave us gifts to serve and support the body. This does not make us any less of a Christian or any less powerful.

The fivefold ministry gifts listed in Ephesians are gifts that represent the authority in the church or body of Christ. Everyone is not called to perfect the Saints and keep the body unified as this takes a special anointing given through these ministry gifts. Let's face it, some of us are just not mature and compassionate enough to gather sheep; we may scatter instead. Those of us who desire to be in authority in the church oftentimes don't have the gifting for it. Wisdom is knowing who we are, knowing our capabilities, and knowing our position within the Kingdom of God.

Looking at this concept in the natural; I worked as a law enforcement officer for over 20 years. I was not trained to be a nurse, EMT, a doctor, or fire fighter although all those are a part of the emergency response/management team. The law enforcement role in that field deals with issues and responsibilities that others do not. If a very bad accident occurred, the law enforcement officer may be responsible for clearing the road, directing traffic so the injured can be served by the other team members or emergency responders.

If someone is trapped in a vehicle, the fire fighters and EMT will bring the "Jaws of Life" to cut them out, while law enforcement works to keep the scene safe. Once the injured is taken to the hospital, it is not the responsibility of the law enforcement officer to treat them. This is when a trained nurse, doctor, or medical professional steps in and does their job to stabilize and save the person.

Similar to the body of Christ, there is team work and order.

I have come to understand that we, as Christians, are all at different levels in our journey, and some are still operating under a curse. When we see an individual struggling in the flesh; we shouldn't judge or ridicule them but help show them the way, the truth, and the life through the love of God. Of course, this can only be accomplished if the individual is honest and willing to accept restoration. We don't necessarily have to talk or preach to an individual; sometimes we can reach people by being effective witnesses; living life based on the truth of God's Word. As we do, we watch Jesus who is the way, truth and life, work supernaturally.

The illustration provided in the previous paragraph shows that we all have a part in saving lives; it is what Christianity is all about. Regardless of what others are doing, look to Jesus; the author and finisher of your faith, (**Hebrews 12:2**). Don't wait on a preacher or confirmation from man, God has chosen you and is calling you to get out of the boat and help a drowning soul, who without your influence, is destined to be lost. Winning souls matter!

1 Corinthians 3:6-7 states that, "*neither is he that plants anything, and neither is he that waters; but God gives the increase.*" Don't get it twisted; men and women are used by God every day to speak into the lives of others but we should never give them a higher status than God. We should never put too much weight or trust in our spiritual leaders. We should be careful not to forget who we are really called to serve and obey; they are human and have struggles just as everyone else does. When God calls us, it is not just for ourselves. When we hear His voice and follow Him, as Moses, David, Joshua, and many others did we will see God do the miraculous in our lives.

1 Corinthians 7:23 tells us that, "we are bought with a price and are no longer our own." We don't do things the way we want, but the way the Father desires. When we are caught up in the world's system, it is so easy to disobey God. We must not allow the world to influence the church, on the contrary, the church should be transforming the world.

If you are a Christian, allow God to use you. King Jesus is seated at the right hand of the Father, and when He returns to get the Saints, I pray that He will not say that He never knew us; due to our disobedience or refusing to follow Him sincerely.

The bible states that we can feed the sick and visit the hungry, but if our hearts are far from Jesus, we have no relationship with Him. Search your heart and motives today. Who is the Father calling you to be? Believers follow God and His Word, unbelievers do not. I believe Jesus is calling for all of us to take up our cross and follow Him, even in the mist of persecution and betrayal. It's time to give our lives solely to Him.

∝ CHAPTER FIVE ∝

A Friend Should Love at All Times

I love the word friendship; it correlates with the word relationship. Both require that two or more individuals be involved. **Proverbs 18:24**, states, "there is a friend that sticks closer than a brother." **Proverbs 17:17 (NLT)** says, "a friend is always loyal, and a brother is born to help in time of need." The Bible is the standard that we use to grow and prosper in life and it sets all of us straight before God and helps us line up with Hs truths.

Many people don't like the Bible for whatever reason, but God's Word will always be alive and exist when nothing else will. **John 1:1** says, "In beginning was the word, the word was with God and the word was God." I believe Jesus will exist forever.

Thinking of the word friendship, I am reminded of the ship that Paul was traveling on, as a prisoner, while going to Rome **(Acts 27)**. Paul reached out as a friend to assist his captors; although they had him bound as a prisoner. I believe Paul knew the concept of sowing and reaping. Paul may have felt betrayed while he was captive but even during this time in bondage,

Paul knew his purpose and did not allow the numerous times he was thrown in jail stop him from living out his destiny in God.

Paul was a changed man as the Lord had captured his heart for His glory. That is what we as people of God should be about; our Father's business. After reading about all the awful things Paul did before becoming a mouthpiece for God; one may say that he got everything he deserved.

Paul was a murderer and, even today, we know of others who have committed vicious crimes and that have been forgiven. We must remember that God is a God of mercy and grace and He doesn't wish that anyone should perish; even the worse criminals.

If we kill our brother or sister when we hate them, it is an act of murder **(1 John 3:15).**

As saints of God, we really need to search our hearts and learn to judge acts and things, not people; unless God gives us this authority. Some may look at Pauls' life and say that he reaped what he sowed, but what about Job? He is described as a blameless man **(Job 1)**.

Job feared God; he walked uprightly and shunned evil but, because of the trials he experienced, he felt betrayed by God, his wife, and especially his friends. The book of Job starts out showing that Job was minding his own business, doing the will of God, day in and day out. Job had a great life as he had seven sons and three daughters, seven thousand sheep, three thousand camels, five hundred oxen, and donkeys, along with several servants. Job was one of the greatest men among the people of the East with an abundance of wealth in family and possessions.

Job was chosen by satan because of his high standard and relationship with God and of course satan wanted to prove a point as he always does in an attempt to prove God wrong; that is why he is no longer in heaven and has lost the battle of death. With God's permission, satan puts Job through a number of tests. Regardless of the hardship, the attacks on his body, and having lost everything; Job continues to stand on the promises of God's Word.

Jobs oxen and donkeys were attacked and carried off by Sabeans. His sheep and servants were destroyed by a fire from God. His camels were carried off by Chaldeans; who also killed his servants, and his children were destroyed by a mighty wind that caused a house to collapse on them.

Job was going through great emotional and physical pain but he refused to charge it against his

Heavenly Father; instead he chose to praise God and continued to honor Him.

Many of us have experienced great pain from our friends, and we desired to charge them and take revenge upon them thinking it would make us feel better. We should remember **Galatians 6:7**, where the Bible tells us, "whatever a man sows, he shall also reap." Some of us have done the opposite of Job. We chose to take matters into our own hands; and felt as though we had a right to get even, but we tend to forget that God is trying to be glorified in and through our lives.

It takes great faith to go through the trials Job experienced, and we find that things didn't get any better. Job may have wanted to ask God if his suffering would ever end. He was afflicted with sores all over his body and looked like death; his wife advised him to curse God and die while he sat scraping himself with a piece of pottery.

Some of you have felt like Job while going through trials and tribulations. Some of you were lied on, while others wanted to give up, "But God". Job didn't curse his Heavenly Father and neither did you. He healed you to shut up the mouth of the enemy! You may be experiencing the pain and suffering that Job experienced; don't curse God and die, bless him and live!

In chapter three of Job; instead of cursing God, Job cursed himself and the day he was born. His three friends sat and stared at him as though some strange thing had happened to him. Not one of Jobs friends thought enough to encourage him in his pain; but they sure had enough in them to discourage him, as they went into mourning for seven days. Mourning is a sign of death and this is how Job was treated, so he began speaking death over his own life. For a short time, Job forgot that he belonged to a God who can do exceeding, abundantly far more than we can ask or think **(Ephesians 3:20)**.

The pain Job endured while being a faithfully devoted servant and friend of God, his wife, and the three friends placed him into a special position with God. All of us have a cross to bear, and yes, while we need the support of friends and family; sometimes they criticize and refuse to help us because of fear or a lack of knowledge. The last thing we need are the type of friends Job had; they continued trying to find fault or a reason why he was going through those trials. Eliphaz; one of Job's friends suggested that he had sinned in the eyes of God and advised him to take the correction so God could heal him.

What do you do when you've have faithfully lived by the word of God and are suddenly stricken with poverty and disease? I believe we should do as Job did, he said, "God allows the good, and the bad."

Job needed and desired the devotion of his friends, but he felt forsaken by all. He continued to plea with his friends as each of them began judging him harshly and unjustly. Bildad, the second friend, chastised Job because his children had been destroyed; once again insinuating that it was because of Job's sin.

Zophar the third friend told Job, he may have been free of sin but he was not pure enough for God and that was why things had happened to him. I admire Job tremendously; he was a loyal friend despite the fact that they were not loyal to him. His friends Bildad, Eliphaz and Zophar constantly belittled him while he was down physically, emotionally, and spiritually; so much so, that he desired that his life be taken.

According to **Proverbs 18:24,** there is a man who sticks closer than a brother and his name is Jesus. Although they verbally attacked him on at least ten occasions, Job remained loyal to his friends and showed how real friendship should be. Job needed comfort, love, and mercy but no one gave it to him, "But God."

God was that friend to Job who stuck closer than a brother **(Job chapter 32)**. God sent Elihu to Jobs' side. Elihu sat and listened to Job complain while his friends ignored him; thinking that there was no help for him. They thought he was guilty and refused to admit to the sin he had committed and which caused his suffering.

Elihu was hesitant to speak because he was the youngest amongst the men, but with the power and authority of God, Elihu begins to correct the four men. God uses Elihu to speak His truth to Job and bring him back into the arms of a merciful and loving God; he reminded Job of who God really was.

Friends will betray us, but we must do as Job did when his friends were sent back to him to get forgiveness, Job blessed them and prayed for them **(Job 42)**. Job reminds me of how Jesus took on flesh and became a servant; he humbled himself and submitted to the cross, and because of his obedience, the Father exalted him above all **(Philippians 2:6-9)**. Job was exalted above all as God blessed him with double of what he'd lost.

The bible gives us several examples of friends betraying or turning their back on one another. Peter is a prime example of a cowardly friend and spiritual brother; he betrayed Jesus after he was arrested and stood before Caiphas, the high priest.

Jesus had already told Peter beforehand that he was going to deny him, but Peter continued to follow Jesus and His accusers from a distance. Peter ended up denying Jesus as previously stated, but not before he tried to reassure Jesus of his loyalty. Similar to some of those we call friends; they may lie and pretend to be with us to the very end. Some individuals may say, "I'm with you no matter what; I got your back; you my home boy or home girl," but at the first sign of trouble they'll tuck tail and run like a coward. Peter had Jesus' back; when he watched Jesus get falsely accused.

It is a shame to go through hell for a friend, as Jesus did for the disciples, but as soon as you need a friend; not one can be found to help with the struggle.

Although true friends seem hard to find; there are those out there that will stick closer than a brother. I am sure some of you have had good experiences with friendships; having someone there when you really needed them.

Back in 1991, both my husband and I became unemployed; we lost everything. Prior to that we had a nice home, nice vehicles, and entertained people whom we thought were our friends. Our home nearly turned into a hotel about once a month. Unfortunately, after we lost everything, those so-called friends were nowhere to be found. We asked if our two children could stay temporarily until we got back on our feet, but was often turned away. Some said I along with the children could stay; turning my husband away, while others said he could stay, but not me and the children.

We experienced this from both sides of our families. The betrayal was brutal and a rude awakening of how people will treat you when you are lost and experiencing hardships. I am thankful for my father taking us in. The four of us slept in the one bedroom he was able to offer until we got back on our feet.

I have witnessed individuals get into legal trouble, get thrown into prison, and gone to battle for their friend who committed the crime with them; but unfortunately, no one came to their rescue. The so called friend(s) or their "homeboy or Nig," (although negative, its used as a positive) "ride or die" partner vanished in the time of trouble.

It is awful to experience false accusations from anyone, but especially amongst brethren or sisters in Christ, and no one comes to your rescue. Jesus stood before the priest alone but he already knew that he would be in this situation, just as many of us know beforehand. Jesus knew what was in Peter's heart as he ate and talked with Peter on a regular basis.

We as human-beings, know the majority of the time what type of people we associate ourselves with, but we remain naïve and hopeful that someone will stand by us when we need them the most. But unfortunately, we are often betrayed when they do not come through for us.

In **Matthew 26:31** Jesus continues to tell Peter what is really in his heart and Peter continues to tell Jesus that he will not deny him. Peter should have realized that he was standing before the "Spirit of Truth," the holy one of all. Peter tried to convince Jesus or perhaps impress him with words, but his heart was far from him. He tells Jesus he would never deny him in **Matthew 26:33-35.**

Peter is not only in denial but he is being dishonest. If a friend is going to betray me, he or she should at least have enough courage to be real with me and not try to convince me that they are with me;

especially when they are not. It is okay to speak the truth about a situation. If you are scared or confused, just say so, or don't say anything at all. It is better to be quiet and slow to speak, quick and ready to hear, rather than make a vow, especially before God **(Ecclesiastes 5:4-6)**. When we make a vow, or promise to a friend, he or she depends on that promise. Failing to fulfill the promise may cause devastation and many other problems.

Working with young people of all ages and observing friendships amongst my adult children; I have seen the devastation and betrayal of friendship that seemed almost impossible to get over.

Suicide due to rejection, school and public shootings, fighting, and unnecessary violence; all because of the hurt of being betrayed by a friend whom they thought would remain loyal and have their back. We should always be true to ourselves as well as to our friends. Jesus knows our heart just as he knew Peter's.

Peter was not the only disciple standing in the temple while Jesus was getting sentenced, all of Jesus' friends were there and not one of them tried to help him.

Jesus was faithful to all of the disciples; He fed them, blessed them, and took away their burdens, yet all of them betrayed him on that day. I know Jesus warned them that this day would come, but one would have thought at least the disciples, as his friends, would have tried to help rather than hide in the crowd; regardless of the consequences.

I am not discouraging friendship, but I am encouraging those of us who call ourselves a friend to someone, to be loyal. We need to stick closer than a brother, as a friend, always be yourself, and be real without trying to impress one another, as Peter tried with Jesus. Peter denied and betrayed Jesus three times verbally and, as professing Christians, we are guilty of doing the same thing or worse.

We betray Jesus as we deny him with our mouth, through gossip, lies, or use of obscenities which shames who God really is. We deny Jesus with our bodies when we commit sins such as adultery, fornication, drunkenness, watch pornography, and commit crimes. We deny Jesus with our hearts as we cultivate envy, strife, evil, jealousy, and internal lusts.

Jesus has done all He is going to do for us. We must make it right with Jesus, who was crucified for our sins, lived Holy in the earth, and left the comforter; the Holy Spirit, who guides and leads us into God's truth.

Betrayal will sometimes manifest amongst friends, those who are dear to you, and to whom you have disclosed secrets and personal issues.

Judas Iscariot appeared to have committed the ultimate crime when he led the Roman soldiers to Jesus' secret place and kissed him to let them know that Jesus was the one, they were looking for. It is a custom for Christians to greet friends and brethren with a holy kiss, but Judas used this act to betray Jesus for thirty pieces of silver. Judas got paid for revealing who Jesus was; an innocent man before Pilate. He may appear to be a greedy coward, but this act was destined to happen. We are so quick to judge the one who betrays, but sometimes it is destined to happen so that Gods glory may be revealed in the one who was betrayed.

Judas was not only a friend, and disciple, but a brother who walked with Jesus. Judas disclosed intimate and private information to the enemies who sought to take Jesus' life. We should never disclose secrets or problems of another individual without their permission, unless of course, the information is to prevent something fatal from happening. We should always remain honest, faithful, and true in our relationships. When we are not able to remain honest, faithful, and true we have allowed the flesh to rule us and cause us to make the worse decision concerning another individual.

Some people disclose vital information about others for various reasons, including money. Disclosing information is a violation of confidence, and revealing secrets is not wise when done to injure or tear an individual down. If a friend who's sinned needs to confess their faults and trusts you enough to confide in you, don't betray them by gossiping. They may never recover and, guess what, their blood may be on your hands.

Mary Magdalene was caught in the sin of adultery. The hypocrites or Pharisees demanded that she be stoned to death for her sin, but Jesus gave her life and she used that life to become a disciplined saint who followed Him everywhere. As friends, we should give life not death. We shouldn't tear anyone down or judge them. In **Galatians 6:1** the bible tells us to, "restore such a one that has been overtaken in a fault in the spirit of meekness, considering ourselves as we may be tempted."

☙ CHAPTER SIX ☙

The Fire Is Necessary

Fire is primarily perceived as harmful but, it can be very useful; both naturally and spiritually.

Fire can destroy a house and all its possessions in less than an hour. It can quickly reduce an entire forest to a pile of ash and charred wood. It is a terrifying weapon, with nearly unlimited destructive power. Fire kills more people every year than any other force of nature. Despite these truths, fire can also be extraordinarily helpful. It provided humans with the first form of portable light and heat. Fire give us the ability to cook food, forge metal tools, form pottery, harden bricks, and drive power plants; it is certainly one of the most important forces in human history.

The ancient Greeks considered fire one of the major elements in the universe, along with water, earth, and air. We can feel fire, see it, smell it, and it has the ability to move from place to place. Uncontrolled fire has become one of the main environmental issues facing the global community, in fact, considering the observed effects it has on land area and biodiversity, it is the most important global disturbance. On a global level, an estimated 150-250 million acres of tropical forests are affected by wildfire annually. Many mature and immature forest trees are killed by high intensity fires annually. In the Amazonian forests for instance, wildfire has been reported to cause high mortality in many useful species with the rate ranging between 3696%. Consequently, fires affect timber supplies from which income and other livelihood needs are generated for most people, particularly, in developing countries (Goldammer, 1999).

In Ghana, (one of the leading exporters of timber in Africa), for instance, wildfires caused more than 4 million dollars of exportable timber in losses from 1982 to 1983. In many cases, wildfire causes heavy financial loss in terms of people losing their homes and property. Wildfires also pollute the air with smoke which causes health hazards and makes aerial communication difficult. The carbon emitted during wild fires contributes significantly to the build-up of greenhouse gases in the atmosphere. The harmful effect of wildfire is very clear and explains why the public generally have the opinion, that fires are always harmful to nature (Goldammer, 1999).

For Some of Us, Fire Is a Necessary "Evil"

Despite the destructiveness of fire, it can be a legitimate land management tool, if carefully timed and used. As a result, the Food and Agricultural Organization (FAO), (2006) projects the idea that there is good fire and should be advocated and supported." However, the dilemma faced particularly by the public, in rural communities, is that fire can be very destructive while at the same time, act as a useful tool in the enhancement of ecosystems. The "right kind of fire" by local people can enhance the ecosystem and their livelihoods. Some fire disturbances play a role in creating certain habitats, favoring the relative abundance of certain species, and maintaining biodiversity – the existence of many different kinds of plants and animals in an environment (Goldammer, 1999).

In Africa and Asia, even though in some case wild fires had been ignited for apparently no valid ecological reasons, the use of fire had been and is still an integral part of land use and livelihood systems. Fire is used for field preparation to burn agriculture on which a majority of the rural people depend upon to meet energy and food needs (Goldammer,1999).

In Ghana during the agricultural activities, the local people use fire to control pests and suppress weeds. Fire is also used to prevent the rottenness of the palm tree and to ensure better taste and an increased yield of wine during palm wine processing. To the hunters, fire is a tool for smoking out game. This tells us some of the ways in which communities use fire to cultivate crops, manage pests and disease, hunt and ensure the availability of non-wood forest products (Goldammer,1999).

In grassland ecosystems, fire is the primary mode of decomposition, making it is crucial for returning nutrients to the soil and allowing the grasslands to sustain their high productivity. Research conducted over the past five decades has revealed that fire not only helps to maintain the ecosystem, but also helps to ensure the availability of quality forage (Trollope and Trollope 1999; 2001).

For instance, it was found that in South Africa and Namibia, freshly burnt savanna areas had new plant growth that provided palatable forage compared to unburnt areas with older grasses. More importantly, the fresh forage will encourage large herbivores (plant eating animals) to move to less preferred areas in order to minimize the overuse of preferred areas which are areas kept short by constant grazing (Trollope and Trollope, 1999).

I have given you many examples of how fire is a necessary evil. Fire is necessary in order to rid our land of un-useful substances that prevent proper growth as well as force helpful resources to help find and supply needs, but it can be our evil if not controlled properly.

Revelation or act of revealing to help understand:

So if large herbivores move from less preferred areas into preferred areas that have been created by fire that has been used properly to prepare the soil to bring forth quality forage (grass and plants that herbivores desire), what does this mean for those living in the area who are carnivores (most of us humans)? I believe it means that all of our needs are met when we allow the purification of the fire in our lives to burn off the impurities, so that growth can take place. When the natural is in order; our land or natural bodies seeking God, we are blessed beyond measure with our Father God; who is a consuming fire.

The second and third chapters of **Leviticus**, explains how the fire gift is a pleasing fragrance to God. Note that the book of Leviticus explains that we should never offer strange fire to God. The fire from within must be pure and created by the Holy Spirit. As previously explained, fire in the wrong hands can be disastrous. It can destroy hundreds of acreage and natural habitat. In addition, strange fire has the potential to destroy us as a people.

In **Leviticus 9:22-24** Aaron lifted his hands over the people and blessed them. After having completed the rituals of the absolution offering, the whole burnt offering, and the peace offering; he came down from the altar, then Moses and Aaron entered the Tent of Meeting. When they came out, they blessed the people and the Glory of God appeared to all the people. Fire blazed out from God and consumed the whole burnt offering and the fat pieces on the altar. The people saw the power of God in Moses and Aaron near the Tent of Meeting, so they cheered loudly then fell down, bowing in reverence.

That same day Nadab and Abihu, Aaron's sons, took their censers, put hot coals and incense in them, and offered "strange fire" to God—something God had not commanded. Fire blazed out from God and consumed them—they died in God's presence.

Leviticus 10:1-2

Hebrews 12:28-29 says, "Do you see what we've got? An unshakable kingdom! And do you see how thankful we must be? Not only thankful, but brimming with worship, deeply reverent before God. For God is not an indifferent bystander. He's actively cleaning house, torching all that needs to burn, and he won't quit until it's all cleansed." God Himself is Fire!

Fire is a necessary evil. We need fire to reveal our path as well as to consume things in our lives that do not belong. Sometimes when fire exposes things in our lives, it drives away that which is unnecessary, such as relationships, occupations, ungodly desires that appear to be good, sin, and many other unnecessary things that are not God's will for our lives.

Oftentimes, if we are not living a life of holiness and total submission to God, we will not understand the fire process we face. Regardless of the process or season we are in, we should always remember to walk with the Lord, trust Him, and never lose faith and hope. The fire process can be very difficult for those of who attempt to hold on to what God is trying to burn up.

What I like about fire, is that it is able to consume bad or evil things that cannot be restored or picked up again in some instances.

Proverbs 6:27 asks, "can a man take fire in his bosom and not be burned?" Of course, this type of fire is a result of sin, which is also necessary. Fire can totally destroy what it attacks or touches; this is a good thing when those things are unholy, ungodly, and useless for our lives.

Fire in both the natural and the spiritual can be perceived as harmful, but if we go through the fire process and allow the power of the Holy Spirit, who is also a source of fire in the spiritual; we can truly enjoy the new life God has already created for us.

1:3-5 What a God we have! And how fortunate we are to have him, this Father of our Master Jesus! Because Jesus was raised from the dead, we've been given a brand-new life and have everything to live for, including a future in heaven—and the future starts now! God is keeping careful watch over us and the future. The Day is coming when you'll have it all—life healed and whole.

6-7 I know how great this makes you feel, even though you have to put up with every kind of aggravation in the meantime. Pure gold put in the fire comes out of it proved pure; genuine faith put through this suffering comes out proved genuine. When Jesus wraps this all up, it's your faith, not your gold that God will have on display as evidence of his victory. ⁸⁻⁹ you never saw him, yet you love him. You still don't see him, yet you trust him with laughter and singing. Because you kept on believing, you'll get what you're looking forward to total salvation.

1 Peter 1: 3-9 (MSG)

It is up to us to walk in the newness of life by accepting Jesus as our Lord and Savior. Sometimes, life brings sorrow, disappointment, and negativity. It can get better if we just trust God; the author and finisher of our faith (**Hebrews 12:2**). God promised to never leave us or forsake us, even when others forsake us. God is present to pick us up again and again as long as we are honest and true about our need for Him. Our flesh will pull and fight against the spirit of the living God, but we must yield ourselves to Him, in order for change to take place for His glory.

We may not obtain everything that we feel we deserve but He has prepared a place for us and just as **1 Peter 5** states; "the day is coming when we will have it all; healing and wholeness." I challenge you to receive complete salvation (deliverance from the power and effects of sin) and go through your fire process so you can be restored.

Restoration: Restore – to give back someone or something that was lost or taken; to put or bring something back into existence or use or to return something to an earlier or original condition by repairing it, cleaning it, etc. (Webster).

An example of restoring in the natural:

An old antique car that has been junked because of accidents, damage, and other outside influences or extremes, can be restored. Automobile restoration is the process of repairing the degraded aspect of an automobile to return it to an overall "authentic" condition. It is to renovate a car without updating or upgrading it by keeping in line with how it would have appeared when first offered for sale.

A complete restoration includes not only repair of the parts that can be seen such as; the body, trim, chrome, wheels, and the passenger compartment. The automobile also has other parts that are not so visible; these include the engine, and engine compartment, trunk, frame, driveline, and all ancillary parts like the brakes, accessories, engine cooling system, electrical system, etc. The ancillary parts support the primary activities or operation of the vehicle, and are very vital to ensure that the automobile can function.

Similar to the ancillary parts on an automobile, we as human beings have ancillary parts which help us function each day. Our heart is our engine; our brain is our trunk. If we truly value an authentic automobile, we do not put any type of fuel, oil, or other harmful items into the engine, nor do we allow just anything into our trunks for fear of damage, contamination, or destruction.

We were created for God's glory and He desires to put good things into us. **Philippians 2:5** tells us to, "let the same attitude and purpose and [humble] mind be in us which was in Christ Jesus: humble, forgiving, loving, sound."

When it comes to automobiles, repairs are made to correct obvious problems, as well as for cosmetic reasons. For example, even if a wheel is covered by a full hubcap, is not seen, and is structurally sound, the tire should be un-mounted and any required repairs performed such as rust removal, straightening, priming, and painting.

Sometimes our minds and heart become corroded, corrupt, and may be a little rusty, but God is able to restore all that the enemy has stolen, and all we have given Him. It's time to give our lives back to Him, since we originally came from Him from the beginning. It is okay to allow our creator to restore us back to originality; pure, holy, and obedient worshippers of God. He has given us power and dominion.

Restoration (original restoration) puts a car in the same condition as it was when first offered for sale. Many antique and rare cars are not able to have a true restoration done because parts may not be available to replace or to fully imitate them; yet with the proper research, they may be restored to an overall authentic condition.

Just like the old antique car; our souls can be restored, regardless of the damages, bad influences, pressures, and wrong decisions. If we allow our creator God, to restore us, He will do it!

I am reminded of Abraham, who was one hundred years old, and Sarah, who was ninety-nine years old. In **Genesis 17**, God promised them a son in their old age but He had to restore them to be able to physically bring forth what He promised. God can restore us back to His original purpose but we must allow him to possess us again (be born again).

[1-2]"There was a man of the Pharisee sect, Nicodemus, a prominent leader among the Jews. Late

one night he visited Jesus and said, "Rabbi, we all know you're a teacher straight from God. No one could do all the God-pointing, God-revealing acts you do if God weren't in on it." *3Jesus said, "You're absolutely right. Take it from me: Unless a person is born from above, it's not possible to see what I'm pointing to—to God's kingdom." 4"How can anyone," said Nicodemus, "be born who has already been born and grown up? You can't re-enter your mother's womb and be born again. What are you saying with this 'born-from above' talk?"*

5-6Jesus said, "You're not listening. Let me say it again, unless a person submits to this original creation— the 'wind-hovering-over-the-water' creation, the invisible moving the visible, a baptism into a new life—it's not possible to enter God's kingdom. When you look at a baby, it's just that: a body you can look at and touch. But the person who takes shape within is formed by something you can't see and touch— the Spirit—and becomes a living spirit. 7-8"So don't be so surprised when I tell you that you have to be 'born from above'— out of this world, so to speak. You know well enough how the wind blows this way and that. You hear it rustling through the trees, but you have no idea where it comes from or where it's headed next. That's the way it is with everyone 'born from above' by the wind of God, the Spirit of God."   *John 3:1-8 Message Bible (MSG).*

Sometimes it seems as though we have been damaged to the point of no return, but with God all things are possible!

²⁶ And they were astonished out of measure, saying among themselves, who then can be saved? ²⁷And Jesus looking upon them said, with men it is impossible, but not with God: for with God all things are possible.

Mark 10:26-27 (KJV)

God restores us from sin, wrong relationships, loss of a love ones, loss due to failures, and wrong decisions. He is all we need to restore us from loss, pain, and hurt. I know sometimes it seems impossible, especially when the enemy Satan replays things back to us over and over again, but with Jesus' help we can make it.

Jesus has gone through all we have to endure in this world and more because, he was betrayed by friends, spit on, disgraced, accused, lied on, and worse of all, hung on a cross to die a death He never deserved. So, when you feel like you don't deserve the pain, suffering, and hurt you may be experiencing, look to Jesus, the "**Author**" – the writer who has already finished the book of our lives. He is the "**Finisher**" of our "**Faith.**"

Looking unto Jesus the <u>author</u> and <u>finisher</u> of our <u>faith</u>; who for the joy that was set before him endured the cross, despising the shame, and is set down at the right hand of the throne of God.

Hebrews 12:2 (KJV)

Hebrews encourages us to live by faith, as many great men and women did throughout the bible. They lived in a realm of faith that we don't often see today.

The fundamental fact of existence is that this trust in God, this faith, is the firm foundation under everything that makes life worth living. It's our handle on what we can't see. The act of faith is what distinguished our ancestors, set them above the crowd.   *Hebrews 11: 1-2(KJV)*

F.O.C.U.S

The true meaning of love and forgiveness was revealed to me through God's Word. I was shown how we should love and forgive; Jesus loved us and gave (not money, possessions, or part of Himself), but His life as He; being humiliated on the cross, whipped with many stripes, and later placed in a tomb. Jesus gave His life so that we can have life, but so many of us take that for granted, living as though He has done nothing for us.

Through Jesus, I learned how to live beyond the walls of fear, let my guards down, and most importantly accept who God made me to be. I am accepted by Him and am not concerned whether anyone else accepts me or not. We can't truly live victoriously without being who we really are. We were created to worship HIM (Jesus), no matter how we feel, think, or are influenced by outside entities. Some of us will take the wise road of redemption and answer the call from God; while others will ignore His call. Don't reject eternal life and enter into eternal damnation by choosing to live in disobedience. We should acknowledge the fact that we were created in the image and likeness of Jesus; we are to walk as He walked **(Genesis 1:27; 1 John 2:6).**

Pursuing His will for our lives is key to walking in divine purpose. Pursue means to, "follow or chase after someone or something." So many of us give up on our dreams, goals and sometimes our lives. God has given each of us a purpose; He has made our calling and election sure. Everyone is not purposed to be a preacher, teacher, lawyer, doctor, etc.; but everyone on this earth is SOMEONE special in the eyes of God.

Many times, we miss opportunities because we desire to be like someone else or we allow other influences to get us off path. I have been a hard worker my entire life and as a student, teacher, entrepreneur, parent, and a wife, I have always encouraged and pushed my family to succeed and fulfill their greatest potential; but regardless of what I do, the choice is theirs. Although I have been distracted many times, I have learned that I must maintain my focus and allow God to push me into who He has called me to be.

No one can make YOU who YOU are supposed to be, YOU must choose to allow Jesus to show YOU, and act upon it without excuse. Jesus knew us before our mothers conceived us **(Jeremiah 1)**. Many of us wonder why some are more successful than others; it is simply because they worked toward it. We must be willing to work hard (not be slothful or lazy) and maintain our FOCUS, like the way of the ant in *Proverbs 6:6*.

Yes, I realize that the favor of the Lord is a factor in great success, but if we are doing nothing, how can He favor us? FOCUS is a key factor. I'd like to share what God showed me concerning FOCUS and how it relates to my life.

F = Faithful, O = Obedient, to the C = Call, that brings U = Unified, S = Success. This acronym reminds me of Jesus who was faithful to the call of His Father Jehovah. Jesus obediently gave His life and was crucified in the flesh. He died for our sins, making a way for us to be unified or redeemed back to our creator; paving the way for our success.

We don't have to search far to find individuals who maintained their FOCUS and lived their lives as Jesus did. Here is a detailed explanation of my previous statement about FOCUS.

<u>Faithful</u> – "To be steadfast in affection or allegiance or loyal." If we reminisce about lives, some of us have had teachers, pastors, parents, and others we learned about in school who were "FOCUSed." Martyrs such as; Martin Luther King, Iranian Pastor Yousef Nadarkhani, Rosa

Parks and others on earth, such as Bishop TD Jakes, Oprah Winfrey, Tyler Perry, and many others we know.

Obedient – "Submissive to the restraint or command of authority or just willing to obey." Obedience in the eyes of God is not doing what everyone else wants you to do, but stepping out and doing His will, just as Jesus did.

Called – The word of God explains it far better than you or I ever could: *⁵But to obtain these gifts, you need more than faith; you must also work hard to be good, and even that is not enough. For then you must learn to know God better and discover what he wants you to do. ⁶Next, learn to put aside your own desires so that you will become patient and godly, gladly letting God have his way with you. ⁷This will make possible the next step, which is for you to enjoy other people and to like them, and finally you will grow to love them deeply. ⁸The more you go on in this way, the more you will grow strong spiritually and become fruitful and useful to our Lord Jesus Christ. ⁹But anyone who fails to go after these additions to faith is blind indeed, or at least very shortsighted and has forgotten that God delivered him from the old life of sin so that now he can live a strong, good life for the Lord.   2 Peter 1:5-9 Living Bible (TLB)*

Unified – "The state of being united or joined as a whole." When we are unified, we are whole, healthy, strong, and usable. Being in tuned with the Father, Son, and Holy Spirit keeps us united; and a unified force is something to be reckoned with. Never try to do life on your own; everyone need's someone.

I love the word of God so much, but there are certain scriptures that captivate me! Here is another one I'd like to share.

¹Behold, how good and how pleasant it is for brethren to dwell together in unity! ²It is like the precious oil upon the head, running down on the beard, the beard of Aaron, Running down on the edge of his garments. ³It is like the dew of Hermon, descending upon the mountains of Zion; For there the Lord commanded the blessing—Life forevermore.

Psalm 133:1-3

I encourage you to be unified and get your blessing from the Lord now; don't wait until you get to heaven! There are individuals recorded in the bible who were obedient to God and received His very best for their lives while they lived. God is waiting on you to unify yourself according to **2 Peter 10: 5-11**. Jesus showed His unity with the Father no matter how hard it got. Remember, trials and tests will always come, but through Christ Jesus, we are more than conquerors; we are successful in Him.

Success – Once again, the word of our Living God always gives us what we need to live successful lives. I know I would not have made it without His Word. Let's take a look in the book of Joshua and see what God says about success.

8This Book of the Law shall not depart from your mouth, but you shall read [and meditate on] it day and night, so that you may be careful to do [everything] in accordance with all that is written in it; for then you will make your way prosperous, and then you will be successful. 9Have I not commanded you? Be strong and courageous! Do not be terrified or dismayed (intimidated), for the Lord your God is with you wherever you go."

Joshua 1:8-9

I want to touch on what the Lord says about the **Book of the Law**. In the natural, if I continually break the law of the land and face the consequences of my actions, it would be nearly impossible for me to live a successful life. I wouldn't be successful in raising my children; because I would be absent from their lives. I wouldn't be successful in my finances because I would constantly have to give it to probation and parole officers. I wouldn't be successful in my marriage because people will only forgive so much before moving on.

In contrast, living according to the will of God, following His law, and living in obedience to the Holy Spirit positions me to be successful in every area of my life. Let me help you understand, it is impossible to follow all of the laws of the Bible as well as in the natural, that is where **grace** and **mercy** comes in. I have experienced **grace** and **mercy** in the court of law, both civil and criminal when dealing with traffic tickets. No matter where I have gone, the Lord has been with me, and He will be with you as you're obedient to His Holy Word.

I don't live a perfect life; neither does any other Christian. When we put our trust in and stand on God's Word, the Spirit will lead and guide us through each day. Another scripture that comes to mind is:

1Blessed [fortunate, prosperous, and favored by God] is the man who does not walk in the counsel of the wicked [following their advice and example], nor stand in the path of sinners, nor sit [down to rest] in the seat of scoffers (ridiculers).

²But his delight is in the law of the Lord, and on His law [His precepts and teachings] he [habitually] meditates day and night. ³And he will be like a tree firmly planted [and fed] by streams of water, which yields its fruit in its season; Its leaf does not wither; and in whatever he does, he prospers [and comes to maturity].

⁴The wicked [those who live in disobedience to God's law] are not so, but they are like the chaff [worthless and without substance] which the wind blows away. ⁵Therefore the wicked will not stand [unpunished] in the judgment, Nor sinners in the assembly of the righteous. ⁶For the Lord knows and fully approves the way of the righteous, but the way of the wicked shall perish.   Psalm 1 (AMP)

Testimonies of FOCUS

The Bible shares stories about many who have overcome pain, discomfort, and betrayal in the most treacherous manner; but who kept their FOCUS and fulfilled their purpose on the earth. Here are a few individuals who chose to lose their lives for the sake of the call.

Jesus – Matthew 26:39; John 6:38

Jesus, the Son of God, endured so much suffering in His physical body during the time he lived on earth. I love the fact that, although He was betrayed by so many who were close to Him, He never backed away from His purpose. Jesus leaned and depended on the Heavenly Father for strength, guidance, and power at the appropriate time.

Isaiah 53:5 says; "Jesus was wounded for our transgressions; he was bruised for our iniquities: the chastisement of our peace was upon him; and with his stripes we are healed."

Be healed today, in Jesus' Name. He has already paid the price for us to live better lives and be all we can be in Him. Imagine if He had not been willing to fulfill His purpose in the earth, where would we be today? The book of Luke explains that, Jesus continues His purpose today, a purpose that includes us knowing that He has all power and desires to share that power with us.

¹On the first day of the week, very early in the morning, the women took the spices they had prepared and went to the tomb. ²They found the stone rolled away from the tomb, ³but when they entered, they did not find the body of the Lord Jesus.

⁴While they were wondering about this, suddenly two men in clothes that gleamed like lightning stood beside them. ⁵In their fright the women bowed down with their faces to the ground, but the men said to them, "Why do you look for the living among the dead? ⁶He is not here; he has risen! Remember how he told you, while he was still with you in Galilee: ⁷'The Son of Man must be delivered over to the hands of sinners, be crucified and on the third day be raised again. ⁸Then they remembered his words.

Luke 24:1-8 (NLT)

Moses (Exodus Chapters 2 & 14)

Moses has a true rag to riches story. He was placed in a basket and put in the hands of Pharaoh; a harsh leader of Egypt. There he had and experienced the finer things in life. The word of God shows the bravery of Moses which led the Israelites out of Egypt and showed Pharaoh how powerful God was. God used Moses to pronounce plagues on the Egyptians. In addition, he had a speech problem but he didn't allow his handicap to interfere with God's command or purpose for his life. He was destined to save the Israelites.

Noah (Genesis Chapter 6:7-22)

Noah is a very inspirational story about man, his trust and obedience to God. After hearing Gods' Word, Noah built an arc and assembled animals two-by-two, saving them from the dangerous flood that followed. Many refused to obey because they were too busy committing sin and not listening to a man of God; who ultimately was able to save his entire family.

Abraham (Genesis Chapter 22:1-17)

Abraham is another example for us; he obeyed God to the very end. Abraham was willing to sacrifice his own son in complete obedience to God's command until an angel stopped him. God provided him with a ram instead. Abraham's story shows the power of sacrifice, and reveals that sometimes what we are looking for and what we want to achieve is possible in ways other than we initially envisioned. Abraham wasn't perfect; he made mistakes and sinned, but God knew Abraham's heart and He kept His promises to him.

David (Chapter 17:32-51)

With nothing more than a sling shot David slew one of the biggest men ever known in Philistine. He went from zero to hero, and although his brothers mocked him, he depended on God to defeat Goliath. David faced many giants in his life, of course some of them he himself created. Although David did not live a perfect life, God remained faithful and kept His promises.

Mary (Mathew Chapter 1:18-21)

Mary, the mother of Jesus provides us with another great example. She was chosen by God and granted divine favor to bring forth the Messiah. Mary's humility and obedience to God is a good model that shows us what submission to the Father looks like.

Job (Job Chapters 1-3)

Job was targeted by satan due to his faithfulness and pure lifestyle before God. Everything about Job was attacked. He lost children, livestock, home, health, and much wealth. Things got really bad for Job. We need to understand that even though things may get bad in our lives, it won't always remain that way. God has a plan for our lives, even at times when the devil comes in like a flood. God bragged on Job, and He will brag on us today.

Joshua (Joshua Chapter 6:15-17)

Joshua, with the assistance of a willing prostitute named Rahab, led the Israelites into one of the most famous battles of all time; the Battle of Jericho. He led a group to the city of Canaan and had them surround the city. Eventually, he called for them to go in and take the city. His leadership ability is a great example, and should encourage us to never give up and face our giants regardless how big they may appear.

15Then on the seventh day they rose early at dawn, and they marched around the city in this manner seven times. It was only on that day that they marched around the city seven times. 16And at the seventh time the priests blew on the trumpets, and Joshua said to the people, "Shout! For Yahweh has given you the city. 17The city and all that is in it will be devoted to Yahweh; only Rahab the prostitute and all who are with her in the house will live, because she hid the messengers whom we sent.

(Joshua 6:15-17)

Jonah (Chapter 1:1-17)

The book of Jonah teaches that it is not wise to run away from our fears, especially when God is commanding us to do something. Regardless of that fact, Jonas feared rejection from the people. God instructed Jonah to call the people of Nineveh to repentance, but because of his disobedience, he found himself in a violent storm while out at sea. When thrown overboard, he was swallowed by a large fish, which thanks to God, saved his life. The story shows that running from your fears doesn't work. Eventually, you'll have to conquer them or they will conquer you.

Esther (Chapter 1:9-13) Esther, fought through much fear but she pushed to do what was right in God's eyes, and became bold enough to speak up on behalf of her people. She helped stop the plan to assassinate the king, and helped save the lives of many Jewish people. Esther's ability to stand on her own and defy those who had so much power in the kingdom goes to show that we have no need to shrink back in the face of fear or danger. Even the richest and mightiest of foes can be taken down when God is in control.

Paul (Acts Chapter 9:3-9; 22)

Saul who became Paul after his new identity gained his FOCUS after he was knocked off his horse; he answered the call of the Father. Paul, became the very thing he once hated; a Christian. He did not only become a Christian, but an Apostle of the Gospel of Jesus Christ. He took on the responsibility and went on to establish churches. Paul went through a lot of rejection, hardship, and physical pain as a prisoner and a foreigner, but he did not allow his past nor what others thought about him to hinder his destiny.

ᘓ CHAPTER EIGHT ᘓ

If You Lose Your Life, You Will Find It

Losing one's life for the sake of living His, is really not as hard as we think; it is a mindset. Jesus is the perfect blueprint or pattern. There was one time in my life when, like some of you, I could care less about what the Bible said. After learning how powerful Jesus was, I wanted to know more about Him and walk with Him.

I discovered that being a Christian means to be Christ-like. When Jesus walked the earth, He experienced all types of betrayal, just as some of us have, however, in those moments He taught us how to forgive and showed us how to live out God's purpose for our lives. As I studied the life of Jesus, I noticed we had certain similarities. For example, Jesus was born in, what society thought was shame, through a virgin, He was rejected by religious leaders, experienced betrayal amongst His own family members and friends, was beaten, abused, and humiliated.

He was called names and labeled by others who did not accept Him, discriminated against as a Jew, and ultimately murdered for no apparent reason. Like

Jesus, when we as a believer's experience death in the natural, we know we will rise again. One day we will join Him in Heaven where He is currently seated at the right hand of the Father.

Jesus conquered death, and if we are brave enough to set aside our way of thinking and sinful living, His victorious authority is made available to us and gives us opportunity to live purposeful lives. However, we must be willing to lay down our lives as we know it, take up our cross, and follow a Holy, Righteous King.

24Then Jesus told his disciples, "If anyone would come after me, let him deny himself and take up his cross and follow me. 25For whoever would save his life[a] will lose it, but whoever loses his life for my sake will find it. 26For what will it profit a man if he gains the whole world and forfeits his soul? Or what shall a man give in return for his soul?

Matthew 16:24-26 (ESV)

You have probably read about the flawless, fruitful life of Jesus. Please understand that I am not without fault. He is perfect, powerful, supernatural, and much stronger than we are. He was destined to go through what He went through." I realize that none of us is the Savior, the Miracle-Worker, or Great Messiah but we are His offspring, His royal priesthood, and a Holy Nation. Let's commit to connect with Him in Spirit and in Truth and strive to inherit the promises of God.

¹¹In Him we have obtained an inheritance, having been predestined according to the purpose of Him who works all things according to the counsel of His will, ¹²so that we who were the first to hope in Christ might be to the praise of His glory. ¹³In Him you, also when you heard the word of truth, the Gospel of your salvation, and believed in Him, were sealed with the promised Holy Spirit, ¹⁴who is the guarantee of our inheritance until we acquire possession of it, to the praise of His glory.

Ephesians 1:11-14 (ESV)

I know you may feel that you have a right to hold a grudge for a number of reasons. For example, toward that boss who fired you for no apparent reason, a religious or worldly organization that rejected you, or a parent who, perhaps, never claimed you. You may feel that you have the right to hate the person who took the life of your love one or friend, your ex-spouse who divorced you for another mate, or the person who abused, raped, or molested you etc.

Sometimes life seems to have dealt us a terrible hand, but no matter the test or trial you have faced, I pray that you would release your heart to forgive and live your life in a way that is pleasing to our Lord. Our Heavenly Father has all of the answers, so why not follow Him and live in obedience to Him? Position yourself to live a blessed life.

If we continue to live the way we want to live, believing we are always right, we will continue to allow pride, selfishness, hatred, unforgiveness, envy, jealousy and strife to rule our lives, and our reward will be destruction.

Proverbs 14:12 says, "There is a way that appears to be right, but in the end, it leads to death." If you have survived the worse of the worse, you have a story to tell. Someone within your sphere of influence, your circle, needs to hear how you overcame the situation by the grace of God. I promise you; you did not do it alone. I know how it feels to be stepped on over and over again. People can really take advantage of you, mistaking your kindness for weakness. At one point, I felt as though I was going to lose my mind; that is why it is important that we have the mind of Christ. Although many things happened in my life, I am responsible for allowing some by not standing firm.

Having His mind will strengthen us and help us to develop a backbone so we can effectively stand for righteousness. Standing for righteousness and being a Christian is very different from being a door mat and allowing people to continue using you like a dish rag. You are much more valuable than that! GET A Life in Christ and allow Him to use you to become better at Life!

Although you are going through or have been through difficult seasons in life you can experience true deliverance, forgiveness, and a fulfilled life in Jesus Christ. **Mark 9:23** states that all things are possible to them that believe. There are many who have gone through adversities and experienced betrayal in life. They are no different than you. God is no respecter of persons (**Romans 2:11-16**).

He does not discriminate and will see you through; including those of you who have operated in the spirit of an assailant, having victimized someone. There is room at the altar for you; you simply need to come clean, stop tripping in pride, and confess your sins. God is faithful to forgive, purify, and cleanse us (**1 John 1:9).**

I am reminded of the two criminals who were crucified and hung on either side of Jesus. One of them repented and acknowledged Jesus as Lord before dying. The Bible shows that Jesus immediately accepted him into the Kingdom and he inherited eternal life; while the other mocked and disrespected Jesus and instead of repenting and gaining eternal life, he received eternal death **(Luke 23:39-43 NIV)**.

If you are unable to understand what Jesus did on the cross, think about the many men and women who sacrificed their lives so that we could live a better life. Some of us have parents, grandparents, and others who have kept the faith and lived holy lives before us. We must come to realize that if we lose our lives for Christ's sake (not speaking of the flesh), we will inherit a life of joy, peace, prosperity, and the richness of God.

Giving our lives to Jesus is simply putting down our own ways, feelings, thoughts, and desires, and taking upon ourselves His ways, thoughts, feelings, and desires. Life can get complicated, especially when things worth pursuing are difficult to attain, but we must continue to pursue until we reach our destiny and fulfill our purpose. *[1]I, Simon Peter, am a servant and Apostle of* Jesus *Christ. I write this to you whose experience with God is as life-changing as ours, all due to our God's straight dealing and the*

intervention of our God and Savior, Jesus Christ.
Grace and peace to you many times over as you
deepen in your experience with God and Jesus, our
Master.

Don't Put It Off

3-4Everything that goes into a life of pleasing
God has been miraculously given to us by getting to
know, personally and intimately, the One who invited
us to God. The best invitation we ever received! We
were also given absolutely terrific promises to pass
on to you, your tickets to participation in the life of
God after you turned your back on a world corrupted
by lust. 5-9So don't lose a minute in building on what
you've been given, complementing your basic faith
with good character, spiritual understanding, alert
discipline, passionate patience, reverent wonder,
warm friendliness, and generous love, each
dimension fitting into and developing the others.
With these qualities active and growing in your lives,
no grass will grow under your feet, no day will pass
without its reward as you mature in your experience
of our Master Jesus. Without these qualities you can't
see what's right before you, oblivious that your old
sinful life has been wiped off the books. 10-11So,

friends, confirm God's invitation to you, his choice of
you. Don't put it off; do it now. Do this, and you'll
have your life on a firm footing, the streets paved
and the way wide open into the eternal kingdom of
our Master and Savior, Jesus Christ.

2 Peter 1:1-11 (MSG)

Making sacrifices in order to serve God is not for the weak, the doubtful, or hypocrite; this is something you cannot fake. God is calling for us to have sincere hearts and love Him with all of our hearts. He is a jealous God, but very merciful, caring, and loving. He will guide us home; never leaving or forsaking us. I am so glad I gave my life to Jesus over 20 years ago, the road has not been easy as I have had to give up what my flesh wanted to do and trust God while following His Holy Spirit.

I encourage you to come to Jesus just as you are. I too was weary, wounded, and sad, but I found in Him a resting place, and **He has made me glad!**

⚝ CONCLUSION ⚝

The attacks we experience in life are necessary sometimes. Webster's Dictionary defines attack as, "to set upon or work against forcefully; to assail unfriendly or bitter words or to begin to affect or to act on injuriously." There are many kinds of attacks, but all attacks are led by two main sources; a spirit of evil which is influenced by Satan and the spirit of divinity; which is permitted by God to show the devil who is truly in control. For example, the test that Job endured.

Attacks are similar to betrayal but they are sometimes allowed by God to purify us, reveal who we are in Him, and to push us into our destinies; ultimately, He gets the glory. I thought the physical, sexual, emotional, and mental abuse I experienced as a child and pre-teen was going to kill me. There were times when I wanted to die; I attempted suicide on many occasions. **"But God"** had a greater plan for my life. After sharing my testimony of having experienced every type of betrayal I have suffered, I hope you understand that betrayal is real, but so is healing.

You may have experienced rejection, humiliation, unfairness, injustice, or pain and suffering at the hands of others, but I challenge you to dig deep within yourself and find your purpose in life. Seek out God's will for your life, and strive to become who you have always desired to be. Ignore the opinions of others, because, most of the time, they don't have a clue who they really are."

Although I have experienced many attacks throughout my life, both as an unbeliever and after I became a Christian; I am reminded of what the word of God tells us in *1 Peter 4:12-13; 12Dear friends, do not be surprised at the fiery ordeal that has come on you to test you, as though something strange were happening to you. 13But rejoice inasmuch as you participate in the sufferings of Christ, so that you may be overjoyed when his glory is revealed.*

Attacks will come because the enemy's motive is always to kill, steal, and destroy. His goal is to get us off course to prevent us from inheriting eternal life and from living lives of abundance while here on earth. Let's remember that all hope is not lost.

My favorite scripture reminds us that we can live lives of abundance regardless of what we go through. God reminds us of this in *John 10:10.*

Attacks will come in many forms, but as we strive to have the mind of Christ, He causes us to be more than conquerors. *1 Peter 1:6-9* encourages us as Christians to keep trusting and depending on Jesus; He will bring us through the challenges we face in life. *⁶Wherein ye greatly rejoice, though now for a season, if need be, ye are in heaviness through manifold temptations: ⁷That the trial of your faith, being much more precious than of gold that perished, though it be tried with fire, might be found unto praise and honour and glory at the appearing of Jesus Christ: ⁸Whom having not seen, ye love; in whom, though now ye see him not, yet believing, ye rejoice with joy unspeakable and full of glory: ⁹Receiving the end of your faith, even the salvation of your souls.*

When we are attacked or experience betrayal, we must be careful of how we allow the attack to influence or affect us. Pay close attention to what spirit is attempting to use you. Many of us are injured as a result of betrayal, whether in our homes, jobs, churches, relationships, or by some other means, but we are not supposed to remain injured. Like me, some of you have experienced several forms of attacks, but I must make this point; just as the enemy has used certain forms of attacks against me, if not careful, he will try to use me to attack others. I am not exempted from being used by the enemy to attack others, and neither are you. This is why we must watch and pray!

When a physical injury occurs to a particular area of our body, that area needs to be nurtured, loved, and sometimes given special treatment so that it can heal and become strong again. Sometimes it requires that we be seen by a physician, a specialist, or another highly qualified person. God allows medical doctors, mental health counselors, and other specialists to assist us in the natural, but we must be mindful that He is the ultimate doctor and He wants to see us healed both naturally and spiritually.

Spiritual, emotional, and mental wounds can only heal properly by applying the word of God and allowing others to encourage, strengthen, and build you up again. When we choose to remain injured, never allowing healing to take place, it can affect our entire body. For instance, our brains constantly remind us of the pain preventing us from focusing on anything else. If our minds are not able to focus correctly, it can hinder the rest of the body from functioning properly. Consider those you may know who suffer with mental illness; this is not to say they are bad, or to speak negatively of them. Life may have knocked them down and, for some reason or another they gave up and remained injured.

When trials and tests come our way, we have a tendency to self-destruct, especially when we have no power working in us. God is an all-powerful and all-knowing God who will never leave or forsake us. When we are the righteousness of God, through Christ Jesus, we can get back up again with the Lord's help. God will surround us with the right people when we rely on Him. I am a living witness that God is faithful! Regardless of the tests and trials, I have come to recognize His faithfulness toward me since January 1992.

For a righteous man may fall seven times and rise again, but the wicked shall fall by calamity.

Proverbs 24:16 (NKJ).

I am reminded of the sword that pierced Jesus' side as he hung on the cross. He was wounded for our transgression, bruised for our iniquities, and the chastisement of our peace was upon him, and by his stripes we are healed (*Isaiah 53:5).* Our sickness, diseases, hurts, and pains were nailed to the cross so we could be set free and no longer forced to live in a state of hopelessness, hurtfulness, or discomfort.

Jesus was betrayed by a brother, but as a result, many lives were saved. He took the persecution with a purpose. I encourage you to take whatever persecution you were previously or are currently facing with purpose, and remember God is Able.

When we are injured and allow healing to take place, we become stronger, accepting the brighter side, and enduring as a good soldier. Murmuring and complaining is not a Christian attribute. Engaging in these only prolongs the agony of being hurt, and allows the pain to take us into a mental, emotional, and spiritual imbalance.

As Jesus hung on the cross, I am sure He suffered tremendous pain, but in spite of the pain, He was still concerned about others. Jesus gives us a pattern to follow. It is who we are in Him and how we choose to live our lives that truly matters.

26As they led Jesus away, a man named Simon, who was from Cyrene, happened to be coming in from the countryside. The soldiers seized him and put the cross on him and made him carry it behind Jesus. 27A large crowd trailed behind, including many grief-stricken women. 28But Jesus turned and said to them, "Daughters of Jerusalem, don't weep for me, but weep for yourselves and for your children. 29For the days are coming when they will say, 'Fortunate indeed are the women who are childless, the wombs that have not borne a child and the breasts that have never nursed.' [30]People will beg the mountains, 'Fall on us,' and plead with the hills, 'Bury us.'

[31]For if these things are done when the tree is green, what will happen when it is dry? [32]Two others, both criminals, were led out to be executed with him. [33]When they came to a place called The Skull, they nailed him to the cross. And the criminals were also crucified—one on his right and one on his left. [34]Jesus said, "Father, forgive them, for they don't know what they are doing." And the soldiers gambled for his clothes by throwing dice.

[35]The crowd watched and the leaders scoffed. "He saved others," they said, "let him save himself if he is really God's Messiah, the Chosen One." [36]The soldiers mocked him, too, by offering him a drink of sour wine.

[37]They called out to him, "If you are the King of the Jews, save yourself!" [38]A sign was fastened above him with these words: "This is the King of the Jews."

³⁹One of the criminals hanging beside him scoffed, "So you're the Messiah, are you? Prove it by saving yourself—and us, too, while you're at it!" *⁴⁰But the other criminal protested, "Don't you fear God even when you have been sentenced to die? ⁴¹We deserve to die for our crimes, but this man hasn't done anything wrong." ⁴²Then he said, "Jesus, remember me when you come into your Kingdom." ⁴³And Jesus replied, "I assure you, today you will be with me in paradise."* *Luke 23:26-43 (NLT)*

These scriptures are given to provide biblical insight and encouragement to those of you who have been victimized and who have experienced betrayal. It is my prayer that you get up and live the life God has intended for you to live; one of wholeness and abundance.

If you've caused pain in someone else's life by being the assailant, realize that the pain you've caused them originates from sin. Surrender and true repentance to the Savior is the antidote for you to inherit eternal life too. Jesus paid the same price for you, and you owe no man anything but love. Everyone on earth has experienced pain and disappointment; some greater than others.

God has made a way for us to be whole, live, and be free from the bondages of satan. The devil uses both men and women to try and keep us in bondage or captivity. It's time for us to forgive ourselves and others.

Some of us have caused great pain to others and we should repent, and attempt to repair through God and the leading of His Holy Spirit, if at all possible. I must admit that I still battle from time to time as a result of the betrayal I have suffered. As previously shared in Chapter 1, because I did not resemble my parents, I experienced a tremendous amount of abuse over the course of about 5 years (from the ages of 7 to 12 years old).

For years, I wondered who my real father was, and at the age 48, I finally discovered the truth, which has been difficult for me to live with.

I shared a disturbing dream with my departed sister, that my deceased uncle was my father. My sister, who was battling cancer at the time, felt that she needed to tell me about the rumors shared amongst family members when we were children. Sharon shared that a rumor of my uncle being my father had been going on for years, but because I was such an active individual and a loner, I never knew about it. I later questioned my parents about the situation.

My parents reunited after being divorced for about 12 years, so I decided to meet with the two of them. When I asked my mother if she knew who my real father was, she stated that I had the same father as the rest of her children, and the domestic violence occurred due to lies and rumors. I asked my mother and the man I believed to be my father if they would take a DNA test. It turned out that he is my real father.

With God all things are possible and I truly believe this. It is up to us as individuals to allow God to do a work on those things that seem impossible to us. We should not allow pride, un-forgiveness, or any other factors to hinder God from doing the work that needs to be done. As a result of the abuse, betrayal, mistrust, and shame, God still has a work to do in my family.

It is time for **Restoration** – Allowing God to restore that which was lost, and by faith, believe His Word. Receive **Revelation** – Insight and instructions from Jehovah by listening to the Holy Spirit, and **Dedicating** – Committing our lives to the Father, all while **Exhorting** – Giving God all the glory, honor, and praise He so deserves, without **Limitation** – As the supernatural power of the Holy Spirit destroys the powers of darkness which attempts to hinder our Christian walk.

Let's face it, some relationships will not be restored because it takes the cooperation of all parties involved. No one can make another person do anything, but we must learn to cast our cares on God and know that through it all, He still cares for us.

As Christians we have a holy calling to show the way, the truth, and life in the way we live. Unbelievers should know that Jesus is the way. It is through repentance and receiving Him into your heart, that the Holy Spirit will show you the way.

All of us have a God given purpose that was given before we were born. Your purpose may be to write a book to encourage someone, preach souls into the Kingdom of God, teach and change the lives of our youth and young adults, sing until shackles are broken, parent a child who will lead nations, feed and clothe the needy, or build businesses and schools. To fulfill our destiny, we must be whole. It is impossible to help someone else when we have not dealt with our unhealed wounds. We must allow Jesus to heal us and set us free in our mind, soul, and spirit.

I love Joseph's testimony in **Genesis 37:17-28**. His brothers threw him into a pit, but when Joseph was freed from the pit, he was able to bring his entire family and many others out of a hole (famine in the land), **Genesis 42-45**.

We can also look at Moses' testimony. He left Egypt for a season but returned to free God's people. Both Moses and Joseph were forced to leave their homes for a season, and during that time they allowed God to restore them. They were able to do the work of the ministry, after **Restoration, Revelation, Dedication, and Exhortation, took place without Limitation.** God gave them the ability to save many lives. The Lord is calling you and me to save many lives, even those who are practicing evil as Joseph's brothers were.

Define and reflect on the following words:

Restoration; Revelation; Dedication; Exhortation and No Limitation.

_____

_____

_____

_____

_____

_____

_____

_____

_____

Prayer is a Key to overcome betrayal!

Let's Pray: Heavenly Father, I pray for the individuals who have read these writings and may be dealing with betrayal in any manner. I pray that he or she connects with you in supernatural and miraculous ways. I pray that they know you have their best interests at heart. Father, you know more about us than we do ourselves. Father, I pray that they stop running from you, slow down, assess the situation, and move forward with the leading of the Holy Spirit. Lord, you know my story of being knocked down so many times, but I thank You that even as my friend is reading this book, you Lord, will not only pick them back up, but restore everything in their lives the enemy has stolen. Lord, let them not learn the hard way but help them to humble themselves under your mighty hand and allow you to direct their path. I pray God that if they do not have a relationship with you, that they would come to trust in you, the Almighty God, who is able to lead and guide them and protect them in every way. **In the Mighty Name of Jesus, Amen!**

☙ NOTES ☙

Goldammer, J.G. 1999. **Environmental Problems Arising from Land Use, Climate Variability, Fire and Smog in Indonesia: Development of Policies and Strategies for Land Use and Fire management.**

Classic Cars Restoration Manual; by Kelley, Marcellus A.: Publisher; Barnes and Noble 2011.

Trollope, W.S.W. and Trollope, L.A. 1999. **Report on the Assessment of Range Conditions and the Fire Ecology of the Savanna Vegetation on the Liwa Wildlife Conservancy in Kenya**-1998: Univ. of Fort Hare, Dept. of Livestock and Pasture.

The Holy Bible in Different Translations: (AMP) Amplified Bible; (ESV) English Standard Version; (KJV) King James Version;(MSG) Message Bible; (NIV) New International Version;(NLB) New Living Bible; (NLT) New Living Translation.

Shealey, T. L. 2010. **The Power to Overcome Fear: Breaking Free from the Enemy's Grip**

❧ DISCLAIMER ❧

I am not a licensed counselor or member of clergy. Therefore, I do not share the information in this book to counsel but to encourage as I share how I was healed and delivered from many things under the power of God-Jehovah. Living for God is a choice. Choosing to allow the Holy Spirit and professional counselors (both natural and spiritual) helped guide me through my life struggles. My advice is for you to seek out the same assistance when working through your struggles. I am not responsible for any actions you may take. All risks associated with your actions remain your responsibility. Thank you for taking the time to read and hopefully grasp what you desire from this book. May God bless you!

About the Author:

Wanda Bishop (Turner) is a native of Houston County, Georgia, and is a graduate of Georgia Military College and the Fort Valley State University. She holds a Bachelor's Degree in Criminal Justice and a Master's Degree in Mental Health Counseling.

Wanda is a retired law enforcement officer with over 24 years of experience. She has served in various capacities, including as a Correctional Officer, a School Resource Officer, and a Deputy/Investigator.

Possessing a gentle spirit, Wanda has been used by God to minister to hundreds of youth and young adults throughout her career in law enforcement.

Wanda enjoys the learning experience, and has taught in both secular and spiritual arenas for over 25 years. Her current assignment is assisting offenders in obtaining their General Education Diplomas and teaching/advising students as a Criminal Justice Instructor for the Technical Colleges of Georgia.

Wanda's most rewarding accomplishments in life are noted as giving her life to Jesus, being married to her husband (Joey) for over 30 years, mothering three children, and fulfilling her role as a grandmother.

She is a faithful servant at, "The Winning Church," in Warner Robins, Georgia. Wanda believes that all things are possible!

Her favorite scripture is **John 10:10,** because she believes that although the enemy comes to steal, kill, and destroy, Jesus came that we may have life and have it more abundantly!